GROWING CHALLENGES FOR AMERICA'S NUCLEAR DETERRENCE

Fred Fleitz, Editor
Michaela Dodge
Eric Edelman
Frank Gaffney
John Hopkins
Peter Huessy
Robert Joseph
Matthew Kroenig
Peter Pry
Mark Schneider

Growing Challenges for America's Nuclear Deterrence
is published in the United States by
the Center for Security Policy Press,
a division of the Center for Security Policy

March 25, 2020

THE CENTER FOR SECURITY POLICY
Washington, DC 20006
Phone: (202) 835-9077 | Email: info@securefreedom.org
For more information, please see SECUREFREEDOM.ORG

Book Design by Bravura Books
Cover Design by Matthew Franklin

Growing Challenges for America's Nuclear Deterrence

Table of Contents

List of Acronyms

ABM	Antiballistic Missile Treaty (1972)
ALCM	Air-launched cruise missile
CTBT	Comprehensive Nuclear Test Ban Treaty
DOE	U.S. Department of Energy
EMP	Electromagnetic pulse
GLCM	Ground-launched cruise missile
IAEA	International Atomic Energy Agency
ICBM	Intercontinental ballistic missile (range over 5,500 km)
INF Treaty	Intermediate-Range Nuclear Forces Treaty
IRBM	Intermediate range ballistic missile (range of 3,000–5,500 km)
JCPOA	Joint Comprehensive Plan of Action (2015 Iran nuclear deal)
KT	Kiloton (explosive yield of 1,000 tons of TNT)
LEP	Nuclear Weapon Life Extension Program
MIRV	Multiple independent reentry vehicle
MRBM	Medium range ballistic missile (range of 1,000–3,000 km)
MT	Megaton (explosive yield of 1 million tons of TNT)
New START	Measures for the Further Reduction and Limitation of Strategic Offensive Arms Treaty (2010)
NDAA	National Defense Authorization Act
NNSA	DOE National Nuclear Security Administration
NNSS	Nevada National Security Site, previously the Nevada Test Site
NPR	Nuclear Posture Review
NSC	U.S. National Security Council
NTS	Nevada Test Site
PTBT	Partial Nuclear Test Treaty (1963)
RV	Missile reentry vehicle
SLBM	Submarine-launched ballistic missile
SNDV	Strategic nuclear delivery vehicle
SSBM	Ballistic missile submarine
SSP	Stockpile Stewardship Program
START	Reduction and Limitation of Strategic Offensive Arms Treaty (1991)
TTBT	Threshold Test Ban Treaty (1974)
WMD	Weapon of mass destruction

Introduction:
Growing Challenges for America's Nuclear Deterrence

By Fred Fleitz

Our nuclear deterrent is nearing a crossroads. To date, we have preserved this deterrent by extending the lifespan of legacy nuclear forces and infrastructure—in many cases for decades beyond what was originally intended. But these systems will not remain viable indefinitely. In fact, we are now at a point where we must concurrently modernize the entire nuclear triad and the infrastructure that enables its effectiveness.

General Paul Selva, Vice Chairman, Joint Chiefs of Staff, 2017

For decades, the United States has been committed to nuclear nonproliferation and eventually abolishing all nuclear weapons. However, we live in a dangerous world with new and growing nuclear threats from U.S. adversaries that require our nation to maintain a modern, flexible, and resilient nuclear arsenal to safeguard American security and the security of our allies until the day comes when America's nuclear weapons can be safely eliminated.

In the Cold War and post-Cold War eras, the U.S. nuclear arsenal has served as a deterrent against large-scale conventional and nuclear attacks on the American homeland, forward-deployed troops, and allies. It also prevented many tense situations between the United States and the Soviet Union during the Cold War from becoming military conflicts that could have escalated into devastating wars and potentially a third world war.

The main purpose of America's nuclear weapons is to deter nuclear attacks by U.S. adversaries. But it also has three other purposes: security assurances to U.S. allies and partners, achievement of U.S. objectives if deterrence fails, and the capacity to hedge against unknown and uncertain future threats.

America's nuclear deterrent is credible because it is robust and diverse. Under the New START treaty, the United States and Russia agreed to limit deployed nuclear warheads to 1,550 each. Including weapons in storage, America has about 6,185 strategic nuclear warheads. Russia's total is estimated to be 6,490.[1] Although this represents an 80% decrease in both nuclear arsenals since the Cold War, it is still enough weapons to serve as a robust nuclear deterrent.

America's nuclear deterrent is resilient and difficult to destroy by enemy attacks because it is diverse, consisting of submarine-launched ballistic missiles (SLBMs), land-based intercontinental ballistic missiles (ICBMs), and strategic bombers carrying gravity bombs and air-launched cruise missiles (ALCMs). The nuclear triad delivery systems include 14 Ohio-class submarines; 400 single-warhead Minuteman III missiles, and 46 nuclear-capable B-52H and 20 nuclear-capable B-2A stealth strategic bombers.[2]

Unfortunately, the credibility of the U.S. nuclear deterrent is increasingly threatened. The United States has neglected its nuclear infrastructure and capabilities. It has failed to adapt and modernize its nuclear weapons and nuclear policy to keep pace with a dynamic and proliferating nuclear environment in which old and new actors are developing advanced nuclear capabilities. America's nuclear arsenal is falling behind technologically and deteriorating while others build.

Although there have been recent efforts to modernize U.S. nuclear weapons and extend their lives well beyond design limits, the deterioration of these weapons is so serious that nuclear technicians have been forced to cannibalize older weapons for parts, sometimes by salvaging parts from weapons on display in Department of Energy museums. America's nuclear weapons expertise is also deteriorating as U.S. nuclear scientists who worked on the development of operational weapons or participated in nuclear tests retire and pass away.

This represents a serious threat to U.S. national security that is growing worse by the day.

In this book, nine national security experts look at the scope of the threats facing the U.S. nuclear arsenal and what must be done to arrest its decline and establish a modern nuclear deterrent capable of protecting the United States and its allies.

In Chapter 2, Dr. Michaela Dodge, a research scholar at the National Institute for Public Policy, opens this discussion by explaining the nature and size of the U.S. nuclear arsenal. Dodge discusses problems with the Life Extension Program (LEP), a program to extend the useful life of U.S. nuclear warheads. Antiquated nuclear warheads present growing challenges facing all legs of the nuclear triad and illustrate the urgent need to modernize America's nuclear program.

In Chapter 3, Dr. Matthew Kroenig, deputy director of the Scowcroft Center for Strategy and Security at the Atlantic Council, discusses popular myths about U.S. nuclear weapons and nuclear weapons policy. Kroenig focuses on false arguments made by those who want to do away with U.S. nuclear weapons immediately and who dispute why the United States must maintain a robust, modernized, and diverse nuclear arsenal.

The urgency of addressing growing problems with the readiness of America's nuclear arsenal is described in Chapter 4 by an expert with exceptional experience in the nuclear field, Dr. John C. Hopkins. Hopkins began his career as a student at Los Alamos National Laboratory and is one of the few living nuclear scientists to participate in atmospheric and underground nuclear tests. In his chapter, "Nuclear Test Readiness: What Is Needed and Why?" Hopkins explains that the United States must urgently resume nuclear testing to ensure the readiness and reliability of U.S. nuclear weapons and how such testing could be resumed.

In Chapter 5, we have reprinted a November 2000 Center for Security Policy Decision Brief by Frank Gaffney, the Center for Security Policy's founder and former president. The decision brief tried to inform the incoming George W. Bush administration about why the United States could not maintain a safe, reliable, and effective nuclear deterrent without nuclear testing. Unfortunately, the problems Gaffney raised to the incoming Bush administration about the reliability of the U.S. nuclear arsenal were not addressed by the Bush or Obama administrations and are worse today. As a result, this decision brief remains as fresh today as it was in 2000.

Defense analyst Peter Huessy provides a tour d'horizon of foreign nuclear programs in Chapter 6. He contrasts the growth in these programs—especially Russia's—with the smaller and deteriorating U.S. nuclear arsenal. Huessy discusses the difficulty of nuclear warhead "bean counting" and how the current and future size of China's nuclear arsenal, the world's third largest, is "an exquisite puzzle."

In Chapter 7, two distinguished arms control experts— Ambassadors Robert Joseph and Eric Edelman—look at the difficulty of forging effective arms control treaties that are in U.S. interests. Joseph and Edelman discuss the flaws of the New START treaty, why the Trump administration withdrew from the INF Treaty, and why a new security environment has rendered long-standing assumptions of nuclear arms control obsolete.

Dr. Mark Schneider, in Chapter 8, discusses the urgency of updating U.S. assumptions about nuclear deterrence and policy in light of new and emerging security threats posed by Russia, China, and other potential adversaries. Schneider specifically calls for the United States to adapt its nuclear arsenal by developing low-yield nuclear weapons in response to changes to Russian and Chinese nuclear strategies.

In Chapter 9, Dr. Peter Pry, a former CIA analyst and director of the United States Nuclear Strategy Forum, explains growing nuclear threats posed by enemies of the United States—especially states with small nuclear arsenals—from devastating attacks on the U.S. electric grid using electromagnetic pulse (EMP) weapons. Pry provides an in-depth analysis of this little-known threat, including how EMP weapons could enable a state like North Korea to launch an attack on the U.S. electric grid that could result in the death of up to 90% of the U.S. population.

And finally, in Chapter 10, I review how the Trump administration's proposals to address growing problems with the U.S. nuclear arsenal in the 2018 Nuclear Posture Review (NPR). This chapter discusses what Trump officials said they will do to update and modernize America's nuclear program and new projects and nuclear weapons spending they have proposed to implement the NPR.

Nuclear weapons are a necessary evil to protect America's security and freedom in today's world. However, politicians too frequently side with nuclear weapons opponents and refuse to adopt the policies required to maintain the readiness of the U.S. nuclear arsenal and adapt it to growing and emerging threats. After decades of such neglect, the American nuclear arsenal is now facing deterioration and our nuclear weapons know-how and doctrine are dangerously out of date. It is our hope this monograph will aid the Trump administration and Congress in taking long overdue action to ensure the reliability and value of the U.S. nuclear deterrent.

U.S. Nuclear Weapons: What Is at Stake

By Michaela Dodge, Ph.D.

U.S. nuclear weapons are unlike any other weapons in the U.S. arsenal. Due to their unique destructive power and lasting consequences of battlefield use, their deterrent value is unparalleled. They fulfill critical U.S. national security missions, including deterring large-scale attacks (conventional and nuclear) against the United States and its allies, helping to achieve U.S. objectives if deterrence fails, and providing a hedge against an uncertain future.[3] Because the United States provides nuclear security guarantees to over 30 allies around the world, these countries have been able to forgo development of their own nuclear weapons capabilities. Some of these allies, like South Korea and Japan, are located in dangerous neighborhoods. They have highly advanced industrial bases and access to the expertise and weapons-grade nuclear material they would need if they decided to build their own nuclear weapons.

This chapter offers a brief discussion of the history of the U.S. nuclear arsenal. It also examines the U.S. nuclear weapons posture, principles that have guided it, and the types of nuclear weapons in the current U.S. arsenal. It concludes by discussing some of the challenges involved in continuing to make the U.S. nuclear deterrent safe, secure, and reliable in the coming decades.

NUCLEAR WEAPONS: A BRIEF INTRODUCTION

Within the national security community, there is little agreement about what constitutes a nuclear weapon. Such disagreement carries important policy implications, such as the following:

- If the United States modernizes nuclear delivery vehicles but does not modernize nuclear warheads, how "new" is the resultant nuclear weapon?
- If the United States modifies an existing warhead design at the margin, is such a modified nuclear warhead a new nuclear weapon and, as the post-Cold War experience teaches us, therefore less likely to obtain congressional support?
- How many components in a nuclear warhead can be replaced without compromising confidence that the warhead will perform as expected?

For the purpose of this chapter, a nuclear weapon is understood to be a nuclear warhead and its associated delivery vehicle. When delivery vehicles range over 5,500 kilometers, it is common to refer to them as strategic.

The definition of nonstrategic or tactical nuclear weapons is murkier and generally refers to nuclear weapons with ranges less than 5,500 kilometers and have relatively smaller nuclear yields. This distinction is a legacy of arms control discussions between the Soviet Union and the United States and has nothing to do with how strategic a nuclear weapon might be on the battlefield. It is clear that lower-yield, short-range "nonstrategic" nuclear weapons can achieve strategic effects if used on the battlefield, which is why they are sometimes referred to as battlefield nuclear weapons.

The United States currently deploys three types of strategic delivery systems and one type of tactical delivery system (See Figure 1). The three types of strategic delivery systems, also referred to as a nuclear triad, are bombers (B-52 and B-2), ICBMs (Minuteman III), and submarines (Ohio-class) with SLBMs (Trident D5). The tactical delivery systems are fighters (F-15, F-16, and dual-capable aircraft that U.S. allies in the North Atlantic Treaty Organization deploy).

The United States currently deploys seven types of nuclear warheads: W78 and W87 for ICBMs, W76 and W88 for Trident D5 SLBMs, the B61 family of nuclear warheads for bombers and dual-capable aircraft, B83 for bombers, and W80 for the ALCM that can be delivered by the B-52 bomber (see Figure 2).

Figure 1: Current United States Nuclear Weapons Delivery Systems

		Type of Warhead	First Deployed	Number Deployed	Estimated Explosive Yield
* 	W78	ICBM H-bomb deployed in Minuteman-III	1979	300	335-350 KT
* 	W87	ICBM H-bomb deployed in Minuteman-III	1986	250	300 to 500 KT
** 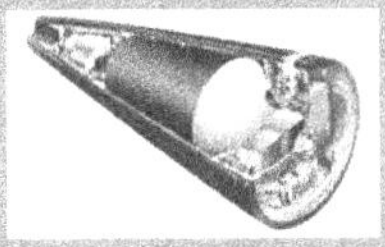	W76	SSBM H-bomb	1978	3,000	100 KT
**** 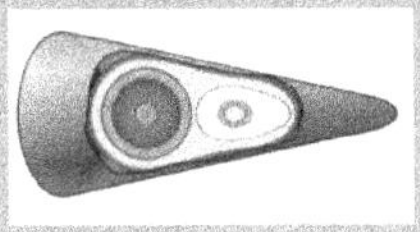	W88	SSBM H-bomb	1989	400	475 KT

	B61	Bomber-deployed H-bomb (gravity bomb)	1968		300 to 400 KT
	B83	Bomber- and fighter-deployed H-bomb (gravity bomb)	1983		1.2 MT
	W80	Cruise missile-carried H-bomb	1983		5 to 150 KT

* Department of Energy/NNSA photos
** Unless otherwise indicated, this information has been authored by an employee or employees of the Los Alamos National Security, LLC (LANS), operator of the Los Alamos National Laboratory under Contract No. DE-AC52-06NA25396 with the U.S. Department of Energy. The U.S. Government has rights to use, reproduce, and distribute this information. The public may copy and use this information without charge, provided that this notice and any statement of authorship are reproduced on all copies. Neither the Government nor LANS makes any warranty, express or implied, or assumes any liability or responsibility for the use of this information.
*** Air Force Photo. Master Sgt. Ken Hammond, October 4, 1989.
**** Wikipedia Commons

Figure 2: The U.S. Nuclear Triad

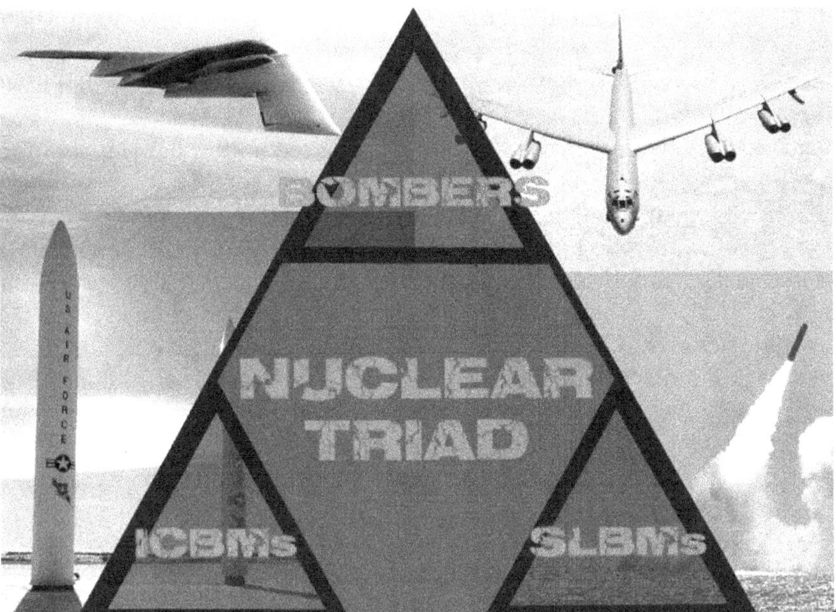

NUCLEAR TRIAD: AN ENDURING NECESSITY

Each leg of the nuclear triad has unique and mutually complementary attributes that make it an essential component of U.S. nuclear force posture. ICBMs are the most responsive. They can be launched within minutes of a presidential order and reach their targets within half an hour. ICBMs are not routinely aimed at targets; they are aimed at oceans to avoid damage in the extremely unlikely case of an accidental launch.

This leg of the nuclear triad is the cheapest to operate but the most expensive in terms of defense. Adversaries wishing to destroy it or defend against ICBMs undergo a complex and expensive process of developing and deploying missile defense systems. Each Minuteman III missile can carry up to three nuclear warheads, although the United States has decided to decrease the number of warheads each missile can carry to one. Uploading additional warheads would require a major effort and additional resources.

Unlike other U.S. nuclear weapons, ICBMs cannot be destroyed by conventional attack due to their hardened silos and dispersal across large areas of the United States. If there were an attempt to attack U.S. ICBMs, there would be no question that an adversary was launching a nuclear attack against the United States. The loss of a bomber or a submarine might be more ambiguous, particularly since these platforms can be destroyed by conventional weapons. Also, because of the way ICBMs are deployed, an adversary would have to use its own nuclear warheads to destroy them, which means these warheads would not be available for other attacks.

U.S. nuclear bombers are the most vulnerable part of the nuclear triad because they do not routinely fly armed with nuclear weapons and are generally more susceptible to an adversary's defensive measures than are ICBMs or submarines. The bombers' prelaunch survivability, however, can be improved in a crisis by arming them with nuclear weapons and dispersing them across Air Force bases. The B-52 and B-2 bombers can carry up to 20 and 16 nuclear warheads respectively. Nuclear bombers are invaluable for signaling and are the only leg of the triad that can be recalled. Their ability to be refueled in-flight gives them unparalleled duration.

Because they can forward-deploy relatively easily, bombers also serve as a visible reminder of U.S. defense assurances to its allies. For example, the United States flew its B-52 nuclear-capable bombers over South Korea in 2013 to signal U.S. commitment to the alliance with that nation while warning North Korea to refrain from further escalating tensions on the Korean Peninsula.[4] Additionally, bombers can perform important conventional missions and in that sense are a truly dual-use platform.

Submarines are the most survivable leg of the U.S. nuclear triad. Because they roam vast swaths of the ocean, they are virtually undetectable by adversaries. U.S. submarines currently carry more warheads than any other leg of the triad. To capitalize further on submarine survivability, the United States maintains a two-ocean fleet, with one submarine base on the Pacific coast and another on the Atlantic coast.

The U.S. Navy has 12 nuclear-armed *Ohio*-class submarines. Even though not all of them are at sea at the same time, this is enough to maintain a continuous at-sea presence, strengthening both survivability and deterrence. An additional two strategic submarines were converted to conventional-only missions to make the United States compliant with arms control reductions. To a limited extent, submarines can be used for signaling purposes, such as by having them visit foreign ports, but this would be an extraordinary deployment for submarines carrying nuclear weapons.

Without the nuclear triad, the United States would be less safe. Successive administrations and Congresses have supported the triad because without it, the deterrent effect of our nuclear posture would be undermined.

"I have questioned the triad and I cannot solve the deterrent problem reducing it from a triad," said former Secretary of Defense James Mattis after being briefed on the importance of U.S. nuclear weapons.[5] Without a triad, adversaries would be able to concentrate their efforts on defeating the remaining components of U.S. nuclear forces, making each one more vulnerable to disruption.

In the future, the United States could find itself easily surprised by negative geopolitical developments. Without the security hedge that the triad provides, responding to such developments in a timely manner without compromising U.S. and allied security would be incredibly difficult.

THE END OF HISTORY?

Today, there is an additional compelling reason for maintaining a nuclear triad: hedging against technological surprise within the U.S. nuclear stockpile. The issue itself has to do with a decreasing diversity within the nuclear stockpile, the methodology by which the United States has chosen to maintain and reduce it over time, significant delays in the modernization of nuclear delivery systems, and post Cold War atrophy of the nuclear complex and its perception. To fully comprehend the difference between the two eras, this section elaborates on approaches to the maintenance of nuclear warheads and delivery systems during the Cold War and contrasts them with approaches the United States has taken in subsequent years.

Following the dissolution of the Soviet Union, the U.S. refocused its strategy on managing Russia's transition from an adversary to a significant but struggling nuclear-armed state with as little general disruption as possible. The spread of nuclear weapon technologies, know-how, and materials became a more prominent concern for U.S. nuclear weapons policy. The United States undertook large bilateral and unilateral reductions of both strategic and tactical nuclear weapons. Following the first Gulf War, U.S. leadership gave precedence to conventional operations such as the war in the Balkans in 1990s and in Iraq and Afghanistan following the 9/11 terrorist attacks. During these conflicts, the United States confronted and has been confronting adversaries that are significantly inferior to it militarily. In this environment, the urgency with which the United States treats and prioritizes nuclear weapons issues has waned.

During the Cold War, the United States maintained a robust and vibrant production complex for nuclear weapons and delivery systems. The country had a large and diverse nuclear weapons arsenal in both nuclear warheads and delivery platforms, particularly on the tactical nuclear weapons level. Leaders in the executive and legislative branches were well versed on the intricacies of nuclear strategy and associated force posture choices. Nuclear deterrence was the primary focus of the Department of Defense, in terms of both the resources and the amount of time its high-level leadership devoted to these issues.

U.S. nuclear warheads were designed for about 10-year lifespans and were regularly replaced by new warheads. Each warhead was mated to its delivery vehicles to ensure that it would work as expected under the extreme duress of a nuclear exchange with the Soviet Union. The nation maintained a vigorous and active warhead testing program to guarantee that new designs performed as expected and that faulty warheads were not introduced into a stockpile, as happened during the U.S. testing moratorium between 1958 and 1962 (faulty warheads were discovered only after the United States resumed nuclear weapons testing). These activities positioned the United States to be flexible, adaptive, and responsive to geopolitical and technological surprises in a timely manner.

All of today's U.S. nuclear warheads are past their original service lives, generally by around 10 years. The B61 gravity bomb has been in the U.S. arsenal since the late 1960s. America's newest warhead, the W88, was first deployed in 1990. Most of the people who designed and fielded nuclear warheads and tested them underground have left government service, are very close to retirement, or have passed away.

The average age of warheads in the U.S. stockpile is about 26 years. That number, however, is skewed because the National Nuclear Security Administration (NNSA), the government agency responsible for ensuring that U.S. nuclear warheads are safe, secure, and effective, resets the age of a nuclear warhead to "zero" after it performs a major modernization effort under the Life Extension Program (LEP).

The LEP is critical for warhead maintenance but does not result in new nuclear weapons. During a LEP, a nuclear warhead is dismantled and aged, faulty components are replaced and reassembled, and then the warhead is certified for an additional 20–30 years. Resetting an age to zero at that point is somewhat misleading because it creates the impression that a new nuclear warhead is being fielded. That is not the case—and not all components are necessarily replaced during an LEP.

The NNSA keeps track of each component of every nuclear weapon, but these numbers are classified. Despite choosing methodology that makes the publicly available average age number seem lower than it actually is, the U.S. nuclear stockpile has never been as old as it is today.

All currently deployed warhead designs predate the end of the Cold War. This means they were designed to deter the Soviet Union. Cold War nuclear warhead designs, for example, prioritized miniaturization and yield-to-weight ratio maximization over safety features. That does not necessarily mean that they are bad designs; however, the U.S. has left other warhead design options largely unexplored even as it faces a strategic environment that is significantly different from the one it faced during the Cold War.

Unlike during the Cold War, the United States currently cannot serially produce plutonium pits, the core components of U.S. nuclear warheads, except for an extremely limited number in laboratory conditions. Plans to reconstitute this capability have been delayed repeatedly. Producing fewer than 80 plutonium pits by 2030 will be challenging because of the potential lack of congressional support and funding to build and convert facilities to support this mission. The United States faces similar production issues with its supply of tritium gas, which decays at 5.5% a year and is a critical component of hydrogen bombs and boosted-fission nuclear weapons.

NNSA facilities also are old and in dire need of recapitalization. About a third of them date back to the Manhattan Project era, and about half are over 40 years old.[6] The NNSA's $10.64 billion Weapons Activities budget for fiscal year 2018 included $2.5 billion for deferred maintenance, indicating that the problem will not be resolved anytime soon.[7] Aged facilities and U.S. policy precluding the testing and fielding of new nuclear weapons designs make it harder to attract and retain talented people to work in this field. A separate but complicating issue is the time it takes to obtain the security clearances required for most nuclear weapons work.

The 2020 National Defense Authorization Act (NDAA) addressed some of these problems by allocating funds to modernize NNSA facilities and $253 million to process plutonium and produce pits. Fred Fleitz discusses the NDAA in Chapter 10.

The NNSA conducts extensive stockpile surveillance and stewardship activities and relies on advanced computer models based on data from previous nuclear weapons tests. These activities, however, are no substitute for yield-producing experiments and a robust nuclear warhead testing program. Such a program could benefit the nation in other ways, as discussed by Dr. John Hopkins in Chapter 3.

If the state of U.S. nuclear warheads paints a bleak picture, the situation is not much better for delivery systems. The first *Ohio*-class submarine was commissioned in 1981, and the last was commissioned in 1997. These submarines will start retiring in the 2030s; the last one is scheduled to be decommissioned in 2042. These ships were originally designed for a 30-year service life. Some will be maintained for 42 years. The Trident D5 SLBM service life was extended to correspond with the *Ohio*-class sustainment timelines.

The Minuteman III ICBM has been in service since the 1970s, with an originally planned 10-year service life. Concerns over the system's survivability prompted the United States to develop the MX Peacekeeper ICBM in the 1980s. Yet the MX Peacekeeper was retired after the end of the Cold War, while Minuteman III is planned to be in service until 2030. This weapons system is so old that further extensions would be unwise given future trends in Russian and Chinese defenses.

The B-2 bomber, the newest leg of the nuclear triad, reached its initial operational capability in 1997, more than 20 years ago. While the bomber is stealthy, that does not mean it is invisible to adversary radars. In fact, sophisticated radar technologies make the B-2 "visible" and therefore vulnerable to adversarial anti-air measures. Following the end of the Cold War, the United States purchased a total of only 21 of these aircraft.[8]

The B-52 bombers were built in the 1950s and 1960s, making them so old that a son, father, and grandfather flew the same aircraft.[9] That, in combination with the ALCM's inability to stay ahead of adversarial technological developments, makes bombers vulnerable to an adversary's air defenses. The United States deploys 46 B-52 nuclear bombers.

The B-21 next-generation bomber will be nuclear-capable, but current plans call for "nuclear certification within two years of declaring initial operational capability."[10] The B-21 should be entering service nuclear-certified rather than waiting to certify later, increasing the risk that additional and potentially costly modifications will be necessary in order to meet requirements for nuclear certification.

The U.S. nuclear deterrent depends on a survivable and resilient Nuclear Command Control and Communications system (NC3). The information architecture will have to be designed in a way that allows for reliable, timely, and unambiguous information transmission under the extreme conditions of a nuclear war. The current NC3 architecture is a legacy of the Cold War that includes using vintage technologies and will have to be modernized concurrently with the modernization of delivery platforms and sustainment of nuclear warheads.[11]

The Trump Administration's 2018 Nuclear Posture Review (NPR) was drafted to address the issues discussed in this chapter. The 2018 NPR is discussed in Chapter 10.

CONCLUDING NOTES

There is no shortage of challenges in the nuclear weapons field, now or in the decades ahead. From questions about U.S. policy hampering the development of nuclear warheads and skill sets, to the need to sustain increasingly aged warheads while modernizing delivery vehicles, to the need to address decrepit nuclear infrastructure and potential lack of key warhead parts, as well as competitors' and adversaries' robust nuclear weapons development efforts, the United States is facing a new nuclear age—a nuclear age for which it may not be prepared.

Myths of U.S. Nuclear Weapons Policy

By Matthew Kroenig, Ph.D.

Few subjects are as important as U.S. nuclear weapons policy and few are as shrouded in myth. While getting U.S. nuclear weapons policy right is of foremost importance to the U.S. and to international peace and security, it is also a politically charged issue. Defense policy professionals understand the essential role of nuclear weapons in U.S. national security, but anti-nuclear advocates believe that nuclear weapons are the most dangerous weapons in the world and that all nuclear weapons, including America's, should be reduced or eliminated. This latter view is reasonable enough and is an expression of a certain set of priorities, but the problem arises when ideologues invent and repeat falsehoods to advance their preferred policy outcomes. To make matters worse, some of these myths have become the prevailing view among many in the academy, the media, and the general public. Unfortunately, there is now a chasm between the true role of nuclear weapons in U.S. national security policy and the (mis)perception of much of the educated public.

The central axis of controversy centers on the proper size and composition of the U.S. nuclear arsenal.[12] For decades, the United States has maintained a robust nuclear arsenal with thousands of nuclear warheads, a variety of delivery vehicles, counterforce targeting policies, and missile defenses. U.S. presidents from John Kennedy to Donald Trump have expressed a preference for nuclear superiority over any possible rival. But critics argue that the United States could manage with a much smaller and simpler nuclear arsenal. They claim that a small nuclear force should be more than enough to deter any adversary and, moreover, the maintenance of a robust arsenal causes many problems for the United States. They argue that U.S. nuclear dominance could undermine "strategic stability" with Russia and China, cause dangerous arms races, spur widespread nuclear weapons proliferation, and deplete the national budget.

This raises a puzzle: Are U.S. policymakers so foolish as to continue self-defeating nuclear policies for multiple decades under both Republican and Democratic administrations? Or is there a logic to

American nuclear strategy that critics do not understand or that they deliberately obscure to advance their ideological agenda?

Fortunately for citizens of U.S. and allied nations, there is indeed a logic to American nuclear strategy. Washington does require a robust posture. Unfortunately, this logic is poorly understood and shrouded in myth. This essay attempts to dismantle several of the most common myths.

MYTH 1: A SMALL ARSENAL IS ENOUGH TO DETER ANY ADVERSARY

Critics of U.S. nuclear policy argue that the United States only needs a small nuclear arsenal to deter any adversary. After all, one or two nuclear weapons going off in Beijing or Moscow should be enough to ruin any Chinese or Russian leaders' day and to deter them from attacking the United States or its allies. Therefore, they argue that the United States can greatly reduce the size of its nuclear arsenal and still maintain deterrence.

There are two primary problems with this argument. First, the United States practices counterforce, not countervalue, nuclear targeting. In other words, the United States plans to use its nuclear weapons against legitimate military targets, not against innocent civilians. If Washington's goal was to threaten to slaughter millions of innocent civilians in Beijing and Moscow, then a few dozen, or maybe even two, nuclear weapons would be enough. But the United States has never possessed a countervalue nuclear targeting strategy. Rather, in the event of a nuclear war, the United States plans to use nuclear weapons against enemy nuclear targets: nuclear missile silos, nuclear submarine bases, nuclear air bases, nuclear command and control centers, and so on.

The United States practices counterforce targeting for two reasons. The first is legal and moral. The law of armed conflict and Just War Theory requires states to distinguish between civilian and military targets in warfare. As a democracy, the United States complies with international law, even when it comes to nuclear war. Other states do not. For example, it is believed that China practices countervalue targeting and, in the event of nuclear war, would aim its nuclear weapons at large cities with the goal of killing as many Americans as possible.

To be sure, nuclear weapons are the most destructive weapons ever invented and even a counterforce strike would result in much death and destruction. However, there is a logical, practical, and moral distinction between a strategy that calls for intentionally slaughtering innocent civilians and one that attempts to hit only legitimate military targets.

The second reason the United States possesses a counterforce targeting policy is strategic: damage limitation. Damage limitation is simply the idea that any enemy nuclear weapons we destroy before they can be used is a nuclear weapon that is not landing on the territory of the United States or our allies. In the event of nuclear war, U.S. leaders would not simply sit back and accept "mutual assured destruction." Rather, they would do whatever it takes to limit damage to the United States and its allies to the greatest extent possible, and counterforce nuclear strikes against an enemy's nuclear forces are a good way to do that.

Counterforce targeting is highly relevant to U.S. nuclear force sizing. With counterforce targeting, the United States needs enough nuclear weapons to cover the nuclear-related targets of its adversaries. To know how much is enough, therefore, one simply needs to count the nuclear-related targets of U.S. adversaries. Moreover, military planners are cautious; it is believed that they allocate more than one offensive warhead to every enemy nuclear target. The precise number is not known publicly, but outside analysts often assume, as a rule of thumb, that two offensive warheads will be assigned to each enemy nuclear target. Indeed, in an unclassified exercise, I did my best to count the nuclear-related targets in Russia, China, and North Korea (America's nuclear-armed rivals). I then multiplied this number by two to arrive at around 2,000 nuclear weapons—which also happens to be the rough size of the U.S. nuclear arsenal today.

If U.S. adversaries increase the size of their nuclear arsenals (as the Soviet Union did during the Cold War) then Washington would need to expand its arsenal accordingly to be able to cover these targets. Contrary to myth, the United States did not engage in an irrational arms race during the Cold War, building more nuclear weapons than it could possibly need. Rather, Washington was simply doing what was necessary to pursue its nuclear strategy.

The second problem with the idea that the United States only needs a small arsenal is that it overlooks the requirements of extended deterrence. All other nuclear powers, including Russia, China, France, India, and others, use their nuclear weapons to deter attacks on themselves. Unlike these countries, the United States does not only seek to deter attacks on itself. Rather, it attempts to deter attacks on the entire free world. The United States extends its nuclear umbrella to over 30 formal treaty allies. The 28 other members of NATO, Japan, South Korea, Australia, and arguably other states depend on U.S. nuclear weapons for their security. Washington made a deal with these countries: Don't build your own nuclear weapons and you can rely on U.S. nuclear weapons for your protection.

Deterring attacks on the entire free world requires a robust arsenal. Nuclear deterrence theorists conceptualize nuclear deterrence as a game of chicken. When political conflicts of interest arise among nuclear-armed states, neither side wants the head-on collision of nuclear war. But neither does either side want to capitulate to a rival on an important geopolitical issue. Instead, they play dangerous games of chicken, or "nuclear brinkmanship," to see who will swerve first. America's extended deterrence policy, therefore, is essentially a promise from Washington to be prepared every single day to potentially play dozens of games of nuclear chicken on behalf of weak nonnuclear allies in the face of formidable nuclear-armed foes.

If you had to play dozens of games of chicken every single day and you had a choice, would you prefer to drive a Hummer or a Prius? It is not that the Hummer always wins, but I would certainly feel safer and behave differently behind the wheel of the more robust vehicle. It is reasonable to expect that the smaller car will tend to swerve first even if a crash would be bad for both. Indeed, I have demonstrated that nuclear-superior states are less likely to be challenged militarily and more likely to achieve their goals when they are challenged. It is not that the nuclear balance of power is the only thing that matters, or even the most important thing, but it does have an influence. Since the United States extends deterrence to the entire free world, it requires a more robust posture than any other state. This feature of U.S. nuclear strategy, more than any other, explains America's recurring interest in nuclear superiority over rivals.

MYTH 2: THE UNITED STATES HAS ENOUGH NUCLEAR WEAPONS TO DESTROY THE WORLD MANY TIMES OVER

Critics of U.S. nuclear policy sometimes argue that the United States has more than enough nuclear weapons to destroy the world many times over. Therefore, the argument logically follows that Washington can afford to cut its nuclear arsenal at very little cost to its security. After all, why have additional nuclear weapons if all they would do is make the rubble bounce? The "destroy the world many times over" line is a catchy and commonly employed talking point (in fact, I once argued this out on the air with a journalist on MSNBC).[13] But it is also false.

We should not downplay the destructiveness of nuclear weapons. They are the most powerful weapons ever invented. A single nuclear detonation in a U.S. city would likely be the worst tragedy in the country's history and a full-scale nuclear exchange among major powers would change the world as we know it.

At the same time, we should not exaggerate the destructiveness of nuclear weapons. Designing good policy requires accurate information. Unfortunately, critics of U.S. nuclear policy often greatly exaggerate the destructiveness of nuclear weapons.

Let us begin with the baseline size of the U.S. nuclear arsenal today. According to the limits agreed to in the New START Treaty, the United States and Russia deploy no more than 1,550 strategic nuclear weapons each. Is that enough to destroy the world many times over?

Since 1945, the nuclear powers have conducted more than 2,000 nuclear explosive tests. The world has not yet been destroyed many times over.

Political scientist John Mueller has written that an enemy attack with 2,000 nuclear weapons would "directly demolish less than five percent of the territory of the United States."[14]

A recent technical study found that it would take 140,000 nuclear weapons to promptly kill 100% of the Russian population.

So, 1,550 nuclear weapons are not nearly enough to destroy everything.

Indeed, there is a contradiction in critics' arguments. On the one hand, they often argue that U.S. nuclear weapons cannot hope to destroy every single Russian or Chinese (or even North Korean) nuclear weapon and, therefore, counterforce targeting and the associated nuclear posture are foolhardy. On the other hand, they argue that the United States has enough nuclear weapons to destroy the entire world. Clearly, both these positions cannot be true.

In sum, 1,550 nuclear weapons are not enough to destroy the entire world, not even once, to say nothing of many times over.

MYTH 3: A ROBUST U.S. NUCLEAR ARSENAL COULD UNDERMINE 'STRATEGIC STABILITY'

A third myth advanced by critics of U.S. nuclear policy is that a robust U.S. nuclear posture could upset "strategic stability" with Russia and China. According to this idea, it is mutual vulnerability to nuclear war that leads to international peace and stability. Therefore, if the United States were to gain strategic advantages through superior offensive nuclear forces or missile defenses, this delicate balance could be upset, resulting in nuclear war.

Critics worry that U.S. strategic superiority could create "use 'em or lose 'em" pressures in Russia and China. Beijing or Moscow, fearing that their nuclear forces could be wiped out in a U.S. first strike, would have incentive to launch their nuclear weapons early in a crisis. Paradoxically, therefore, the United States is safer the more vulnerable it is to Russian and Chinese nuclear weapons.

This argument may seem plausible at first, but it rests on a couple of fallacies. First, the United States possesses both first strike and second-strike capabilities. Early theoretical concerns about "use 'em or lose 'em" were in situations in which both sides possess a first, but not a second, strike capability. If both countries can shoot first and disarm the opponent, then both sides have an incentive to shoot first. But that is not the situation we are in today. The United States also has a second-strike capability. So even if Russia and China fear that their forces might be vulnerable to a U.S. first strike, they cannot hope to disarm the United States by striking first. The United States would simply absorb the attack and retaliate with a devastating second strike. So, Russia and China have no incentive to intentionally launch a nuclear war, even if the U.S. possesses nuclear superiority.

Second, "use 'em or lose 'em" is a false dichotomy. If the choice were truly between being disarmed in a nuclear attack or starting a nuclear war, then Russia or China might be tempted to start a nuclear war. But these are not the only options in international politics. States have a wide variety of policies to choose from, including backing down, seeking diplomatic off-ramps, and living to fight another day. Indeed, my research has shown that time and again, states in inferior strategic positions tend to submit to their superior opponents.

MYTH 4: U.S. NUCLEAR MODERNIZATION WILL CAUSE DANGEROUS ARMS RACES WITH RUSSIA AND CHINA

Perhaps the most widespread myth surrounding U.S. nuclear policy is that U.S. efforts to strengthen its deterrent will cause an arms race with Russia and China. This is the lazy trope used by many journalists whenever there is news of new U.S. strategic capabilities. As the *New York Times* reported when the United States tested a new intermediate-range, conventionally armed missile in 2019, "Are we headed for another expensive nuclear arms race?"[15]

The answer is no. An arms race assumes that Russian and Chinese decisions about their own strategic postures are driven primarily by the strategic postures of the United States. But Russian and Chinese decisions about their strategic capabilities are often made irrespective of the United States. The United States tested an INF-range missile because China already had hundreds if not thousands of missiles in this category and because Russia began testing and deploying these missiles years ago.

If there is an INF arms race, Russia and China have completed several laps while the United States stretched on the sidelines.

Similarly, Russia is building several new nuclear systems without prompting from the United States. Moscow is building a new nuclear submarine drone and a nuclear-powered nuclear-armed cruise missile. From reading the U.S. press, however, one would get the impression that only U.S. capabilities can start an "arms race."

Arms race arguments also assume that U.S. adversaries have the capability and will to engage in a strategic arms competition with the United States, but this is rarely the case. The United States possesses the largest and most innovative economy on the planet. North Korea and China have opted out of trying to match the United States warhead for warhead. Additionally, the Soviet Union tried for decades during the Cold War to keep pace with the United States and it helped to bankrupt their economy.

A basic international relations theory lesson would also be helpful. According to international relations theorists, there are two primary models of arms racing: the spiral model and the deterrence model. In the spiral model, there are two states that only want to be secure. One state builds up its military forces to protect itself. This needlessly threatens the other state, which then needs to build up its forces to protect itself, and so on. The result is a spiral of arms buildups, hostility, and possibly conflict despite the lack of any underlying conflict of interest. This is the model of international politics that most journalists seem to have in mind when reporting on strategic issues.

The second model of international politics, however, is the deterrence model. In this model, there is an aggressive or "greedy" state. It is building up its forces to revise the international status quo, gain power, and possibly attack its neighbors. In this scenario, if the other state does not build up its forces, then deterrence will fail, and the first state will engage in aggression. In the deterrence model, therefore, arms racing is the best policy. When there is a dangerous rival threatening you and your allies, you need to build forces to deter conflict.

So, the first question one must answer in the real world is, are U.S. adversaries greedy or security-seeking states? If they are merely trying to protect themselves, then a strong U.S. strategic posture can lead to spirals of hostility. If, on the other hand, they are greedy states looking to aggress against U.S. allies, then improvements to U.S. strategic capabilities strengthen deterrence and contribute to international peace.

Given that Russia and China have both used military force to take contested territory from their neighbors in recent years, it is hard to argue that they are merely security-seeking states. A failure by the United States and its allies to build sufficient defenses, therefore, will most likely result in further aggression. Critics of U.S. nuclear policy often write as if arms racing is inherently bad, but unfortunately, sometimes it is the best policy.

MYTH 5: U.S. NUCLEAR WEAPONS SPUR NUCLEAR PROLIFERATION IN OTHER STATES

Critics of U.S. nuclear policy often argue that unless the United States makes drastic reductions in the size of its nuclear arsenal, it will cause other countries around the world to build nuclear weapons. They claim that if the United States—the most powerful conventional military force on Earth—needs nuclear weapons to defend itself, this sends the message that other less powerful countries also need nuclear weapons for their security. In addition, they claim that the United States has promised to disarm in the Nuclear Nonproliferation Treaty (NPT). If the United States does not make progress toward this goal, they claim, then the NPT will be weakened, and other countries will withdraw from the treaty and build their own nuclear weapons.

Again, these arguments seem persuasive at first, but they are in fact fallacious. Put yourself in the shoes of a leader thinking about building nuclear weapons, say Iran's Supreme Leader or Kim Jong Un in North Korea. What is on your mind? You are likely thinking about whether (a) nuclear weapons would advance your country's security, (b) you have latent industrial capacity to build nuclear weapons, (c) you can get nuclear assistance from other more advanced nuclear states, (d) the international community will crack down with tough economic sanctions or military strikes, and (e) if the international community does crack down, you can withstand the pressure. With all these relevant considerations on your mind, where does the size of the U.S. arsenal enter? Is Iran's Supreme Leader thinking, "Well, if the United States has 1,550 nuclear weapons, then I will build my own nuclear weapons. But, if Washington cuts its arsenal to 1,000 nuclear warheads, then I will abandon my program"? This simply is not plausible.

Other defenders of this position would say that it is not the potential proliferators themselves that we can affect, but the other countries we need for nonproliferation enforcement. When Washington wants countries like India, South Korea, and Japan to reduce purchases of Iranian oil and gas to put pressure on Iran, for example, they will be more likely to help if they see that the United States is committed to nuclear disarmament, including through its own posture decisions. Again, this is superficially plausible, but also incorrect. These countries' decisions on nonproliferation enforcement are driven by their relationship with the

United States, fear of U.S. secondary economic sanctions, concerns about Iran's behavior, domestic economic dependence on foreign energy imports, and many other factors. But, once again, it is implausible to think that their decisions are being affected by the size of the U.S. nuclear arsenal.

Indeed, I have conducted systematic statistical research showing that there is no link between the size of the U.S. nuclear arsenal and the proliferation and nonproliferation behavior of other states.[16]

If anything, a robust nuclear posture stops nuclear proliferation. As explained above, the United States extends deterrence to over 30 formal treaty allies. Without those nuclear security guarantees, it is very likely that many U.S. allies, including Germany, Japan, South Korea, and others, would possess nuclear weapons today. In the future, a weakened U.S. nuclear deterrent could encourage Poland, Taiwan, Vietnam or other vulnerable frontline states to reconsider their nuclear options. Indeed, a robust U.S. nuclear posture should be counted among the world's greatest bulwarks against the spread of nuclear weapons.

MYTH 6: U.S. NUCLEAR WEAPONS ARE TOO EXPENSIVE

The final myth of U.S. nuclear weapons policy is that nuclear weapons are too expensive. In fact, the United States has plans to modernize its nuclear forces over the next 30 years and the nonpartisan Congressional Budget Office (CBO) has estimated that the cost of this modernization program will come to over $1 trillion. Critics have argued that we should not spend that much money on doomsday weapons that we will likely never use. Rather, we should spend it on more usable conventional weapons or invest in life and not death, such as in roads, schools, and hospitals.

One trillion is certainly a large number, but let us put it in perspective. Over the course of 30 years, this comes to about 5% of the U.S. defense budget. Moreover, several past U.S. secretaries of defense, including, most recently, Secretary Mattis, have stated that nuclear deterrence is the most important mission of the U.S. Department of Defense. Is 5% of the budget too much to spend on the Pentagon's most important mission? Reasonable people can disagree, but to me it seems like a good value. Indeed, as Obama's Secretary of Defense Ash Carter stated, "Nuclear weapons don't actually cost that much."[17]

CONCLUSION

This essay addressed several of the most common myths about U.S. nuclear policy. These myths are often invoked by those who believe nuclear disarmament should be the primary objective of U.S. nuclear policy. They use these arguments to discredit longstanding U.S. efforts to design a strategic force for the primary purpose of defending itself and its allies and deterring international conflict. If the above myths were indeed true, then U.S. strategic policy would be foolhardy indeed. It would mean that the United States builds and maintains a large strategic nuclear force that provides zero benefits and comes with many unjustifiable costs.

As this essay has demonstrated, these arguments are widely shared beliefs, but they are not true. U.S. nuclear strategy requires a robust nuclear force and such a force comes with an acceptable cost.

This is not to say that the United States must always and forever maintain a robust nuclear posture. If Washington decided to change its strategy, then it could also change its posture. If Washington, for example, wanted to abandon the laws of armed conflict and adopt a countervalue nuclear targeting policy aimed at slaughtering innocent civilians, then it could afford to cut the size of its arsenal. Or, if Washington wanted to follow a more isolationist policy, abandon its allies in Europe and Asia, and allow former allies to build their own nuclear arsenals, resulting in widespread nuclear weapons proliferation, it could also cut the size of its arsenal.

So long as the United States wants to continue to play its traditional international leadership role, uphold international law, and contribute to geopolitical stability and international peace, it will continue to require a robust nuclear force.

Nuclear Test Readiness: What Is Needed and Why?

By John C. Hopkins, Ph.D.

In a national emergency, could the United States safely test a nuclear weapon tomorrow? Is Nevada still the obvious place to conduct a nuclear test? In this article, I contemplate the challenges of reviving—and possibly relocating—America's nuclear testing program.

The United States has not conducted a nuclear test since 1992. I am one of the dwindling number of people left who participated in U.S. nuclear weapons tests. I participated in five tests in the Pacific in 1962 and some 170 tests in Nevada in the 1960s through the 1980s. I witnessed another 35 or so nuclear tests. Because I know something about the skills, equipment, facilities, and infrastructure necessary to field a full-scale nuclear test, I have grown increasingly concerned about the steady degradation of U.S. nuclear test readiness—that is, about the capability of the United States to test its nuclear weapons should the need to do so arise.

In fact, my review of assessments made by the Department of Energy (DOE) of U.S. nuclear test readiness leads me to question whether the DOE has, after almost 25 years of being out of the testing business, any realistic appreciation for what nuclear testing involves or how to stay prepared to do it again within 24–36 months, as legally required by Presidential Decision Directive 15 (1993).

STARTING UP OR STARTING OVER?

Nuclear testing as we did it at the Nevada Test Site (NTS, now called the Nevada National Security Site, or NNSS) was a profoundly large and complex endeavor. The 1,375-square mile site sits about 65 miles northwest of Las Vegas and was used from 1951–1992 for 928 atmospheric and underground nuclear tests. Back then, the U.S. nuclear enterprise was not just a program; it was a nationwide industry that required more than 100,000 highly trained, experienced people. During the Cold War, peak testing years, we averaged about one test a week and NTS employed more than 7,000 people on-site.

According to the NNSA—the organization within the DOE obligated to maintain U.S. test readiness—much, if not most, of the equipment and technology required for nuclear testing in the past has not been adequately maintained, is obsolete, or has been sold or salvaged. More importantly, the knowledge needed to conduct a nuclear test, which comes only from testing experience, is all but gone. Currently, no federal funding directly supports maintaining test readiness.

In sum, there is essentially no test readiness. The whole testing process, whether to conduct one test or many, would have to be reinvented, not simply resumed.

If the United States decided tomorrow that it wanted to test a weapon in the nuclear triad, the path to do so (safely) would be long and complicated, and it would look something like this.

WHERE COULD WE CONDUCT A NUCLEAR TEST?

This answer largely depends on how soon the president orders a test and wants it to happen.

In an emergency—such as the need to evaluate the safety, security, and performance of an existing but questionable nuclear weapon design—I assume we would test underground and not abrogate the 1963 Limited Test Ban Treaty that bans tests in the atmosphere, oceans, and outer space. I also assume we would adhere to the 1974 Threshold Test Ban Treaty, which limits tests to a maximum yield of 150 kilotons of TNT. (Nuclear yield is the amount of energy released, expressed as a TNT equivalent. A kiloton is 1,000 tons, so the treaty limits yield equivalents to no more than 150,000 tons of TNT.)

At first look, the NNSS is the obvious place to resume testing. But this is far from certain. More than 800 of the nuclear tests there were conducted underground in deep shafts (or sometimes tunnels). More than a dozen shafts still exist that might be serviceable.

However, since the last underground test in 1992, nearby Las Vegas has exploded in population. In 2015, the city had 630,000 residents, 360,000 more than in 1990. (In 1951, the year testing began, the population of Las Vegas was about 25,000.) In 2015, the greater Las Vegas metropolitan area had a population of more than 2.1 million—1.4 million more people than in 1990.

More people equal more buildings. Today, Las Vegas has more than 50 buildings over 328 feet tall (25 stories high), including the 1,150-foot Stratosphere Tower, the tallest observation tower in the United States.

Additional questions would need to be answered by planners prior to an underground test at the NNSS. What is the maximum yield that could be fired at the test site without causing seismic damage to Las Vegas infrastructure and its surrounding communities? Will recent construction be resistant to seismic energy following a 150-kiloton blast?

Will future maximum test yields have to decrease as the local population increases?

HOW BIG OF A TEST COULD BE CONDUCTED IN NEVADA?

The answer to this critical question lies in accurately predicting the seismic effects of a nuclear test's yield at NNSS on Las Vegas and the surrounding communities.

Detailed geologic and safety analyses of the current Las Vegas area would be required to develop a prudent estimate of the upper limit of the yield. Ultimately, scientific judgment would play a key role in this estimate, but that judgment would rely on recommendations coming from relatively young scientists and engineers who have no experience in nuclear testing.

Figure 3: Height of Notable Structures Compared to Depth of Nuclear Testing

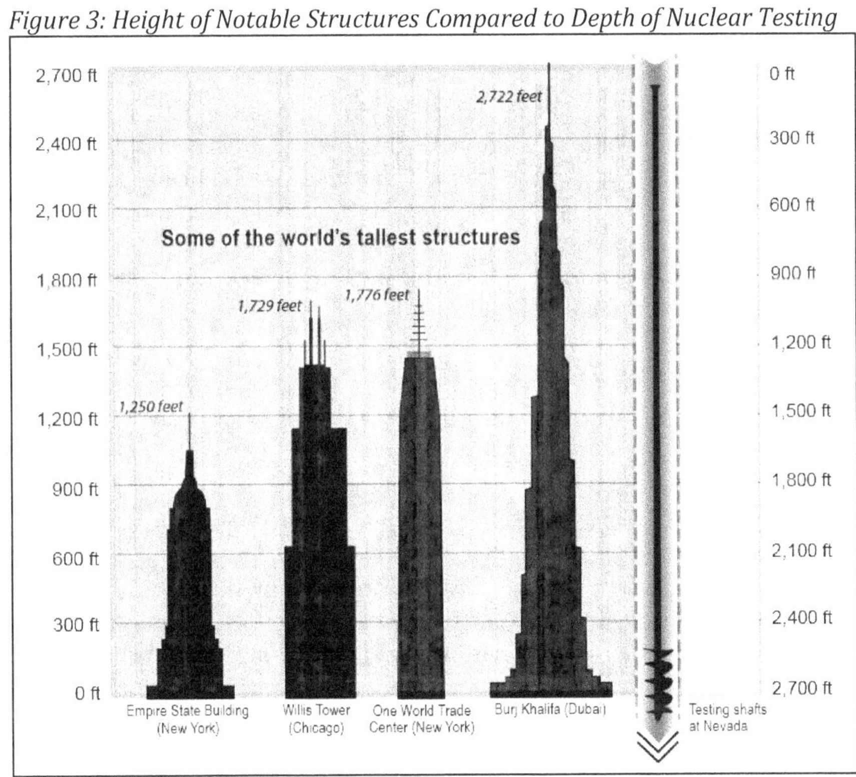

During the period of underground testing at the NTS, 13 shots were fired at a depth of 3,000 feet or more; six of those were fired at least 4,000 feet below the surface.

Previously, the Atomic Energy Commission (the predecessor to today's DOE) hired an engineering contractor to analyze the structural integrity of buildings in Las Vegas and their vulnerability to ground motion due to nuclear explosions. Test readiness means that buildings, especially skyscrapers and the greater metropolitan infrastructure, would have to be carefully evaluated. Reconstituting this program would require a major effort.

Throughout the testing period, Las Vegas construction workers were notified when an upcoming shot might cause significant ground motion. The reasoning was that such shaking could be unsafe for workers in exposed locations, particularly at high-rise construction sites. Mines in the region were also notified of ground motion that could conceivably cause damage and injury. A new plan to communicate a testing schedule to the civilian workforce would have to be developed.

HOW CAN SEISMIC EFFECTS BE MITIGATED?

"Decoupling" an explosion can mitigate seismic energy. Decoupling involves testing the nuclear device in an underground cavity large enough to absorb—and thus reduce—the force of the blast. Higher yield explosions require larger cavities. Larger cavities require significantly more time, effort, and cost to excavate. The National Academy of Sciences estimates that, depending on geology, a cavity 121 feet in radius requiring the removal of nearly 7.5 million cubic feet of material would be needed to decouple a 3-kiloton test.

HOW CAN A NUCLEAR TEST BE CONTAINED?

The risk of venting, the leaking of radioactive materials from the ground into the atmosphere, must be minimized. U.S. underground tests were designed to prevent venting. In the past, preventing venting was a major challenge for the geologists, engineers, and construction crews at the test site.

Previously, we selected a location and designed the emplacement shaft to contain a yield that was usually about 10% larger than the expected yield. Successful containment depended on studying the geology at each test location—no two test locations had the same geology—to see if the shaft could contain the test after successfully stemming (backfilling) the shaft.

Figure 4: Setup of the Testing Location

Gas-blocked cables are shown here laid out in an s-shape prior to an underground nuclear test. The cables were lowered down-hole along with a giant steel rack that contained the test device and multiple diagnostic sensors used to gather data. The cables relayed the data up to trailers (shown here in the foreground and parked at a safe distance from the detonation) containing the data recording equipment. In the background is a 10-story tower assembled around the giant rack and directly over the test hole. The tower was disassembled and removed in sections after lowering the rack but before the detonation. The tower was then reassembled over the next test hole. (Photo: DOE)

To be effective, stemming required an experienced expert to layer a special brew of adhesive epoxies (which are no longer available) and various types and sizes of gravel. This mixture was then packed around specially designed gas-blocked cables that were used to transmit command-signals down-hole and send scientific data up to the surface. The cables were gas-blocked to prevent any venting up through them, and I doubt whether these special cables are still available. If not, they would have to be redesigned, tested, and manufactured anew.

Each test's stemming was unique, varying with the test's predicted maximum yield and a thorough study of the geology surrounding the shaft. Stemming was both a science and an art, and few experts with stemming experience can still be found.

All the geophysical tools that were, over many years, designed, built, tested, calibrated, and fielded at the NTS specifically to collect samples and characterize the geology no longer exist. The designers and operators are long gone, too. The laboratory analysts who had the skills and experience to evaluate the samples for grain density and for compressive and sheer strength are likewise long gone. Today, the kind of detailed geologic and safety analyses and yield predictions needed to successfully contain a nuclear test would depend upon people who have no nuclear testing experience.

Even with stemming, the risk of venting could never be reduced to zero. Dangerous surprises (for example, unknown cracks, caves, or moisture) might be lurking right next to the area of geologic sampling. One dramatic failure was the huge venting from the 1970 Baneberry shot, which was caused by undiscovered geological problems at the test site.

To be prudent, we always assumed that massive venting might occur. So, we were in touch with all of the potential downwind residents and had helicopters ready and evacuation plans for every rancher out mending fences and every sheepherder tending to his flock—anyone who might be at risk the day of a test.

WHAT WOULD IT TAKE TO PLAN AND IMPLEMENT EMERGENCY EVACUATIONS CLOSE TO THE NNSS TODAY?

What about sticking to lower-yield tests? The NTS was originally chosen for nuclear testing largely because of its remote location at that time. Once testing went underground, we soon discovered that, fortuitously, the geology is nearly ideal for reducing venting and seismic impact—thus limiting negative impacts to the environment caused by higher-yield (more than 10 kiloton) tests.

The water table at the NTS is deep: 1,300 feet at Yucca Flats, where low-yield shots were traditionally fired, and 2,000 feet at Pahute Mesa, which was used mostly for high-yield shots. The overlying layers of weak, porous tuff and alluvium provide dry pore space to trap radioactive gases. The site's easily crushable porous tuff also significantly absorbed the seismic waves of our higher-yield tests.

But surprisingly, and perhaps counterintuitively, low-yield nuclear tests are harder to contain at the site. In part, this is because the crushable tuff doesn't crush as well from lower-yield tests, meaning that the risks of venting increase. So, risks to the environment actually loom larger. Successfully stemming a lower-yield test is more difficult.

These risks can be addressed by burying a low-yield test as if it were a higher-yield test, but this approach requires a level of time, effort, and expense commensurate to conducting a higher-yield test. Therefore, the better approach is to design an effective containment plan at the nominal depth required for the lower yield, assuming that the expertise necessary to do this is available. Clearly, the assumption that focusing on lower-yield tests gets us any closer to nuclear test readiness needs a closer look.

WHAT ALTERNATIVES EXIST FOR NUCLEAR TESTING BESIDES NNSS?

If not in Nevada, then where? If challenges preclude using NNSS, an alternative testing site would be required. Amchitka Island in the Alaskan Aleutian Islands would probably be the next-best candidate site. Three tests were fired there: Longshot (1965) and Milrow (1969) by Los Alamos and Cannikan (1971) by Lawrence Livermore.

However, not much infrastructure is left on the island other than an airstrip and perhaps two holes that were, at one time, meant for future nuclear tests. All the buildings are gone. The lack of infrastructure, great distance, and remote location make Amchitka vastly more expensive and inconvenient than working in Nevada. The island also has a wretched climate with dense fog and rain. In addition, Amchitka is now part of the Alaska Maritime National Wildlife Refuge and going back there to test would certainly be concerning to environmentalists and Native Alaskans.

Do other locations exist? Studies of alternative sites have been made in the past, but like at Amchitka, political, cultural, and natural environments have changed since those studies were undertaken. New, costly, and time-consuming assessments would need to be done. Should the nation be actively searching?

CRITICAL SKILLS AND ASSETS REQUIRED FOR NUCLEAR TESTS

As might be imagined, many unique and critical assets—facilities, materials, and equipment, much of which is not commercially available—must be available to successfully execute an underground nuclear test. Tests fired in shafts, for example, involved a nuclear device and experimental equipment installed inside a tall steel structure called a rack, which was lowered down-hole. The racks, which were designed and fabricated specifically for each shot, could be almost 10 feet in diameter and more than 100 feet tall. The assembly of all the experimental equipment required that the rack be surrounded by a tower built of prefabricated units and large enough for the scientific and engineering staff to work on-site at all levels of the rack.

The Los Alamos racks were fabricated at Los Alamos and shipped to Nevada for installation of the scientific equipment. The nuclear test device was installed as the last step before the rack was carefully lowered down-hole on cable harnesses, which were also fabricated at Los Alamos. Livermore's racks were fabricated by a contractor in Las Vegas and were lowered using drill pipe, a completely different technique. Pros and cons exist for each option. How to revive these critical, complex, and costly skills for a future nuclear test must be addressed.

Figure 5: Environmental Impacts—Subsidence Craters at Yucca Flat

Subsistence craters—depressions on the surface that occur when the roof of the blast cavity collapses into the void left by the explosion—still mark the surface of Yucca Flat, where many underground nuclear tests were conducted at the NTS. The size of subsistence craters depends on the yield of the device, the depth of the test, and the geological characteristics of the surrounding soil. (Photo: DOE)

THE STAKEHOLDERS

After two decades without testing, who would be the current stakeholders, and what would their roles and responsibilities be? What are the challenges to negotiating new and complex chains of command and responsibility? The White House, DOE, NNSA, Department of Defense, and State of Nevada would be among the key stakeholders, along with more than a dozen other government organizations such as the Defense Nuclear Facilities Safety Board, the Defense Threat Reduction Agency, the Environmental Protection Agency, the U.S. Public Health Service, the National Oceanic and Atmospheric Administration, the State Department, and Congress. Because the United Kingdom's nuclear strategy is closely allied to ours, I presume the U.K. would participate where its national security interests are involved. Imagine the difficulties of getting all these gears to smoothly mesh together.

Although Los Alamos, Livermore, and Sandia national laboratories would supply much, if not most, of the technical staff, most of the testing personnel would come from a wide range of outside organizations. Contractors for the NNSA would do almost all construction, related logistics, and other support work. These contracts might include providing test diagnostic support (once supplied by Edgerton, Germeshausen, and Grier, Inc., which no longer exists) and the architect/engineering support (once supplied by Holmes & Narver, Inc., which is still in business). The now-defunct Reynolds Electrical & Engineering Company provided the heavy construction services, including operating cranes and drilling shafts, some of which were more than 4,000 feet deep. The technology and expertise to drill new, large-diameter, deep, and straight testing shafts would almost certainly have to be recreated. Significant economic and technological challenges would arise if the pre-moratorium-drilled shafts need to be cleaned of debris or pumped dry of water. Seemingly mundane perhaps, but vital, are requirements for housekeeping and security. Currently, a few of these requirements are being met at the site (to accommodate staff conducting subcritical experiments, for example), but they would have to be expanded to accommodate a much larger operation. Other services—for example, recreational programs and facilities—would have to be completely reinvented.

THE LABS

I would strongly urge the three nuclear weapons labs to form one unified test program, with each lab having well-defined responsibilities and clear accountability. (Previously, each lab had its own testing programs.) I would recommend pulling together a steering committee of the labs' key staff, including weapons designers and engineers, diagnostic scientists (such as physicists and radiochemists), geologists, engineers (civil, mechanical, and electrical), and logistics and travel personnel. A scaled-down version of this type of organization probably exists today as a result of the subcritical tests currently conducted in Nevada, but it probably lacks all the expertise needed to execute a full-scale nuclear test.

I would suggest that the labs' test program leaders place high priority on selecting an archivist. Perhaps not obvious, the rationale for the archivist is this: In developing the testing organization and structure, there will be many questions about what, how, and why things were done in the past. Laboratory archivists could make answering those questions much easier, assuming that the old testing files are stored somewhere in the labs and can be found.

MAKING NUCLEAR TEST READINESS A PRIORITY

With every day that passes, the United States grows more out of practice and out of resources—including the most important resource: people with experience, who are critical to nuclear testing. The testing process, whether for one test or for many, would in many respects have to be reinvented, not simply restarted, which would take longer than 36 months. Past practices will help identify *what* to do but not necessarily *how* to do it—primarily because science, technology, politics, and culture have changed so dramatically since 1992.

A resumption of nuclear testing would involve a large, expensive, and complex program. Because the United States has little left from its previous test program, and essentially no test-readiness program, the time delay following the decision to resume testing—because of a loss of confidence in the stockpile or due to a geopolitical crisis—would, in my opinion, be dangerously long.

Let's not wait to find out how long.

The United States Cannot Maintain a Safe, Reliable, and Effective Nuclear Deterrent Without Nuclear Testing

By Frank Gaffney

Editor's note: The below issue brief by the Center for Security Policy's founder and former president Frank Gaffney was published in November 2000 to advise the George W. Bush administration on the U.S. nuclear posture. Regrettably, Bush officials did not heed Mr. Gaffney's warnings, which have proved prescient and still apply today.

Center for Security Policy Decision Brief, November 29, 2000.

One of the early agenda items for the next president will be the matter of what to do about the —an accord that was negotiated and signed by Bill Clinton in 1996 but considered so fatally flawed that it was rejected by a majority of the U.S. Senate in 1999.

The CTBT will require priority attention even if, as seems likely at the moment, the 43rd president is not Al Gore—who explicitly promised, if elected, to try to ram the CTBT through the Senate as his first order of foreign policy business. George W. Bush, who expressed his opposition to the treaty when it was being considered by the Senate, must nonetheless address this accord as soon as possible for two pressing reasons:

1) Notwithstanding blithe assurances by the Clinton-Gore Administration and other CTBT proponents, the U.S. nuclear deterrent cannot be sustained indefinitely without a resumption of nuclear testing; and

2) the administration has stealthily proceeded with the treaty's implementation as though the Senate had approved its ratification rather than rejected it. As a result, the United States is being inexorably drawn into legal, technical, and political arrangements that will make it difficult, if not as a practical matter impossible, for the next president to resume nuclear testing if and when he decides to do so.

THE *NEW YORK TIMES* CONFIRMS CRITICS' WARNINGS ABOUT STOCKPILE STEWARDSHIP

Incredibly, the gravity of the problem confronting the nation's nuclear forces was documented in a lengthy November 28, 2000, *New York Times* article.[18] The following are among the more noteworthy points made in the course of the *Times* documentation of the inadequacies of the administration's so-called Stockpile Stewardship Program (SSP).

The SSP is not up to the job.

Since [1992, when the United States began a unilateral moratorium on nuclear testing], the Nation has evaluated the thousands of warheads in its aging arsenal in a program called science-based stockpile stewardship, using computer simulations, experiments on bomb components and other methods to assess the condition of the weapons without actually exploding them.

Program officials have been confident that the stockpile is safe and secure and that the stewardship program can fully maintain the weapons. Now, however, some of the masters of nuclear weapons design are expressing concern over whether this program is up to the task. Concerns about the program take a variety of forms, including criticisms of its underlying technical rationale and warnings that the program's base of talented scientists is eroding....

A stewardship program with no testing is "a religious exercise, not science," said Dr. Merri Wood, a senior designer of nuclear weaponry at Los Alamos National Laboratory. Dr. Wood said that as the weapons aged, it was becoming impossible to say with certainty that the stockpile was entirely functional. "I can't give anybody a safe period," she said of the possibility that some weapons could become unreliable. "It could happen at anytime.

Dr. Charles Nakhleh, another weapons designer at Los Alamos, said doubts about the stewardship program were widespread among weapons designers. "The vast, vast majority would say there are questions you can answer relatively definitively with nuclear testing that would be very difficult to answer without nuclear testing," he said.

The arsenal was built for a limited shelf-life.

The program is a fiendish technical challenge, and even its backers concede that science-based stockpile stewardship can never offer the certainty of the big explosions. The thousands of bombs in the stockpile are highly complex devices. Each is made up of a forest of electronics and missile components surrounding a sort of atomic fuse, or "primary," that holds chemical explosives and a fission bomb containing a fuel like plutonium. In addition, there is a "secondary," whose thermonuclear fusion reaction is set off when the primary explodes.

Most of the weapons in the stockpile were not built with longevity in mind. It was expected that they would be replaced by a continuing stream of new and improved designs, checked in tests until weapons production abruptly stopped in 1992. But the basic design of the newest of the bombs, a version called the W88, received crucial tests in the 1970s and fully designed by the mid-1980s. Production of the weapon ended by 1991. The oldest of the bombs date from 1970.

Uncertainties abound.

Assessing the changes can be bewilderingly difficult. The degradation turns symmetrical components shaped like spheres or cylinders into irregular shapes whose properties are a nightmare to model in computer simulations. Inspectors, who typically tear apart one weapon of each design per year and less intrusively check others, find weapons components deteriorating in various ways because the materials age, and because they are exposed to the radioactivity of their own fuel. Even tiny changes in those materials can lead to large changes in bomb performance, weapons designers say.

We're whistling past the graveyard.

Supporters of the program say that regular inspections of the weapons will turn up any serious problems as the stockpile ages and that those problems can be addressed. "You'll get the warning bell and you'll know what to do," said Dr. Sidney Drell, a physicist at the Stanford Linear Accelerator Center, who led a study in 1995 that underlies the stewardship program. Drell said he remained optimistic about scientists' ability to limit that element of doubt, which he called "genuine and serious."

But other experts at the nation's weapons laboratories are challenging this view. Designers say the sensitivity of the bombs to slight changes means that age could modify the bombs so that they do not work as they are supposed to. While program supporters believe those problems can be found and fixed, virtually everyone agrees that if any major redesign is needed, those new bombs could not be certified as reliable under the current program.

Dr. Harold Agnew, a former director of Los Alamos, said that "to consider putting those things in the stockpile without testing is nonsense."

Decline is inevitable.

"In a blink, I would prefer to go back to testing," said Dr. Carol T. Alonso, a weapons designer for 20 years who is now assistant associate director for national security at Lawrence Livermore National Laboratory in California.

Thomas Thomson, a weapons designer at Livermore, said that under the current program, "I think you just accept the fact that you're going to have a decline" in the reliability of the stockpile. "You try to make it as gradual as possible," he added.

We have no comparable experience by which to be guided.

Even with all the [advanced diagnostic tools the SSP is supposed to provide], critics say, crucial questions about the performance of aging bombs must still be answered directly by data from old tests. Because bombs this old were never tested, they say, computer simulations cannot definitively determine the seriousness of new types of changes caused by continued aging....

Serious questions about the operation of the stockpile program are being heard at all three of the major American weapons laboratories: Los Alamos, Livermore and Sandia.

Our nuclear program is suffering from brain drain.

As a result [in part of security investigations at the labs and their repercussions] according to officials at the weapons labs and at the Energy Department, which runs them, there has been a flight of scientific talent and a decline of top-flight applicants, problems exacerbated by a rise in lucrative job offers from the private sector. Weapons experts say the frustration over tighter security procedures comes at a particularly unfortunate time, as the scientists who designed and tested the weapons in the stockpile try to pass their knowledge and experience to new caretakers before retiring or dying. "We have a five-year window to make this transfer," Dr. [Michael] Bernardin, [a senior weapons designer at Los Alamos], said.

Remanufacturing is not an option.

One way to get around all these criticisms of the program and still avoid testing, some scientists outside the laboratories say, would be simply to "remanufacture" new, nearly exact replicas of existing weapons in the stockpile and replace them on a regular basis as they age. Neither very much science nor underground testing would be necessary.

But Dr. Jas Mercer-Smith, a former weapons designer who is deputy associate director for nuclear weapons at Los Alamos, said that was easier said than done, since many manufacturing techniques of the past were no longer available, and the copies could in reality be significantly different from the originals. Without the sophisticated scientific analysis of the stockpile stewardship program, he said, nuclear experts could not be sure what effects the changes might have.

We need to modernize the stockpile.

Dr. Bernardin of Los Alamos said possible new military needs, anything from building nuclear-tipped missile interceptors to replacing an existing weapon completely if it became too old to function, could someday require entirely remade designs as well.

Supporters of re-manufacture insist that no new designs are needed because the nation's nuclear deterrent is sufficient. If they are needed, however, the uncertainties and complexities involved in any new designs would inevitably require underground tests, and not just computer simulations, several weapons designers said. Those complexities, Dr. Wood of Los Alamos said, mean that even existing designs are now coming into question. "If this was somebody's hair clip, I wouldn't mind as much," she said. "But it's not."

Changing facts on the ground.

In one of the most brazen of its many affronts to the U.S. Constitution, the Clinton-Gore administration spent millions of dollars and untold man-years on the implementation of the Comprehensive Test Ban Treaty in the year following its rejection by the Senate. Thanks to the work of U.S. government agencies, official representatives to various international forums and special interests, this country has provided critical technical expertise and other forms of support essential to the operations of the multilateral organization being set up to backstop the CTBT.

President Bush will inevitably be confronted, as a result, with the argument that this entity has been established with U.S. assistance and requires its continued leadership in order to function. The temptation will be great to go along by avoiding a public repudiation of the treaty and the domestic and international criticism sure to follow.

It would be a serious mistake to accede to this pressure, though. The more the Comprehensive Test Ban Treaty is institutionalized and the U.S. is implicated in its work, the more illegitimate will appear actions by this country needed to safeguard and modernize its deterrent forces but that contravene the letter and/or the spirit of the CTBT. This back-door Clinton-Gore ratification of the CTBT must not be allowed to go unchallenged.

THE BOTTOM LINE

As long as U.S. national security depends upon even a single nuclear weapon, the nation, and its potential adversaries, are going to have confidence that it will work if it is needed to do so—and, no less importantly, that it will not work under all other circumstances. There is no getting around it: Periodic, safe underground testing is required to have and maintain that confidence.

Candidate Bush pledged to conduct a comprehensive review of America's nuclear posture. In addition to weighing carefully the wisdom of further deep reductions in the U.S. arsenal and the idea of de-alerting such weapons as remain, President Bush must redirect the nation's policy toward nuclear testing.

Specifically, he should make clear—as President Reagan and Mr. Bush's father did in the past—that nuclear testing is a necessary part of maintaining a credible American nuclear deterrent, not an evil to be curtailed. The United States will not test any more often than is absolutely necessary, but it will conduct such tests when they are deemed necessary.

Mr. Bush should, accordingly, renounce the CTBT and secure its formal removal from the Senate's calendar of pending business—the only way to establish that this fatally flawed accord will not be allowed to undermine U.S. security in the future.

It would have been a public service had the *Times* seen fit to blow the whistle before the election on the inherent inconsistency between a permanent, "zero-yield" ban on nuclear testing and the requirement to maintain a safe and effective American deterrent for the foreseeable future. Still, given the *Times* editorial board's vociferous support for the CTBT, however, and its castigation of Republican Senators, many of whose criticisms have now been vindicated by this article, it is little short of a miracle that the paper ran it at all.

An Overview of Foreign Nuclear Weapons Programs

By Peter Huessy

In popular opinion, the world's nuclear arsenals are primarily located in the United States and Russia, and as such that is where most of the attention is focused. Numerous assessments, from the Stockholm International Peace Research Institute (SIPRI), the Federation of American Scientists (FAS), CNN and others put these arsenals at roughly 6,500 warheads each, with the next largest arsenals in the 100 to 300 range, comprised of the nuclear forces of the United Kingdom, France, Pakistan, India and China. Thus 90% of the world's nuclear weapons are in the hands of the Russia and the United States.

These bean-counting exercises are distorted, primarily because they assume U.S. warhead levels are comparable to those of Russia, which they are not. This distortion leads to three more shaky assumptions: (1) the United States has an obligation to "stop the arms race," which it has been complicit in starting; (2) the United States has to show restraint in nuclear modernization with an eye toward implementing the policy goal of moving toward nuclear abolition; and, at the very least, (3) the United States must remain in the New START strategic arms treaty of 2010, which is characterized as the only remaining restraint on the building of nuclear arsenals.

All of these implied "policy" choices are cleverly included in many of the news stories about such nuclear bean-counting exercises, often as a subtle reminder to the American people that it is the United States that must restrain its own strategic nuclear modernization effort and show leadership, for example, by lessening the role of nuclear weapons in U.S. deterrent policy, including adopting such nuclear policies as "no first use."

IMPLICATION OF ERRONEOUS NUCLEAR BEAN-COUNTING NARRATIVES

The commonly held narratives or assumptions about the size and purpose of the Russian and Chinese nuclear arsenals are wrong, certainly misleading, and if continued to be accepted, will significantly harm America's national security.

Many of these assumptions are rooted in wishful thinking, especially the outdated and erroneous notions once held about détente and arms control adopted by the U.S. nearly half a century ago, when the Soviet

Union pursued arms control and détente as ruses to help it gain strategic superiority.

Of most significance is the widely held idea that Russia and China share the American view of nuclear weapons as last-resort, retaliatory elements only, as opposed to seeing nuclear weapons as everyday diplomatic instruments of coercion and blackmail to be used to secure the fruits of aggression.

Nuclear war fighting—as the actual or threatened use of nuclear weapons is often described—is in fact the accepted policy of Russia since at least 1999 and of China more recently. The Russian assumption is that the U.S. will rigorously avoid a possible nuclear confrontation and stand down in the face of actual or threatened nuclear aggression, including the limited use of nuclear weapons, rather than come to the protection of our allies and friends and risk the exchange of nuclear weapons.

In this way, if successful, Russia and China can illustrate to the world that the United States will no longer protect its friends, and as such can hardly be considered the "leader of the free world."

NUCLEAR DÉJÀ VU ALL OVER AGAIN

This approach was exactly the Soviet strategy throughout the Cold War, and now it's back. The election of President Reagan in 1981 thankfully interrupted the Soviet ambitions, but those Russian objectives have returned. Meanwhile, at home, American opponents of nuclear modernization and realistic approaches toward Russia and China have staked out policy positions remarkably similar to the Soviet active measures themes of the 1980s against the Reagan buildup.

The Reagan administration's nuclear modernization success holds a key lesson for today. The deployment of American intermediate nuclear force (INF) missiles in Europe and the Peacekeeper ICBM deployment in the U.S. did upset Soviet plans. Détente supporters in the U.S. academic, entertainment, and media community supported not Reagan's strategy, but a "nuclear freeze," an idea put forward by the U.S.S.R. in 1979.

In fact, at President Reagan's first White House press conference, the initial two questions were about whether the new administration accepted "détente" and whether it would abide by SALT II, the new Strategic Arms Limitation Treaty that former President Carter had withdrawn from Senate consideration following the Soviet invasion of Afghanistan. President Reagan responded that he hardly considered the SALT II treaty "arms control" when it allowed the Soviets to build up to over 10,000 deployed strategic nuclear warheads, or détente since it was simply a cover for Soviet aggression. Needless to say, the collective reactive gasp of the assembled Washington press corps, audible when the president laid out his "peace through strength" vision, understandably panicked the protectors of the conventional wisdom of détente and arms control. In response, a massive disinformation campaign began opposing Reagan's nuclear deterrent initiatives. Most common were very large, almost daily European crowds marching against the deployment of our INF missiles despite the completed deployment of Russian SS-20 missiles aimed at Europe measuring in the thousands of new warheads. These demonstrations were later determined to be largely organized and funded as Soviet active measures operations.

However, as it turned out, the Reagan INF and Strategic Arms Reduction Talks (START I) strategies defeated the freeze supporters, upending their attempt to seize the high ground of arms control. Reagan's proposed revolution of reductions of nuclear arsenals, coupled with a companion effort to modernize our entire nuclear enterprise, flummoxed the Soviets and their allies, who had assumed arms control could be used to stop American nuclear modernization. Coupling robust American nuclear modernization efforts with new energetic missile defense research, Reagan undid Soviet efforts to achieve nuclear superiority. He knocked the SALT process into oblivion and ended the assumption that arms control meant unilateral American disarmament and failure to keep a strong deterrent. Reagan undid Soviet strategy with the successful deployment of the highly controversial U.S. Pershing intermediate-range ballistic missiles and ground-launched cruise missiles (GLCMs) in Europe, and the simultaneous push for an alternative zero-zero option of eliminating all such American and Soviet INF missiles. These actions wrecked the Soviet campaign to divide and dissolve NATO and played an important role in speeding the peaceful end of the Soviet empire.

However, with the end of the Cold War and dissolution of the U.S.S.R., the United States relaxed its watchfulness. Under both political parties, the U.S. fell into a blindness toward Russia that ultimately led to the assumption that a more cooperative Russia, even under Vladimir Putin, would be available to pursue a security "reset." Meanwhile, the policy establishment in Washington simultaneously swallowed the Chinese Politburo description of Beijing's growing military power as simply a benign "peaceful rise" with which the U.S. should cooperate.

The resulting American nuclear procurement holiday, in which the U.S. virtually stopped its nuclear modernization, was also coupled with a holiday from nuclear strategy and policy assessments. As a nation we fell into sloppy thinking about the nuclear balance, particularly that the arsenals of Russia and United States were comparable. We remain now caught in this same environment in which the media, Hollywood, and academia assume that the U.S. is leading a nuclear arms race, that our nuclear arsenal needs only, at best, modest modernization, and that Russia and China are merely reacting to American military pressure, seeking only to counter-balance U.S. conventional superiority and unilateral military adventures.

IS NUCLEAR BEAN-COUNTING THAT SIMPLE?

Although the Russian and United States nuclear arsenals are measurable to the degree that "nuclear beans" can actually be verified, today only a fraction of the warheads can be counted. They are not similar in range or scope and are not uniformly controlled by the New START treaty in which so much faith has been placed as a measurable governor of the Russian nuclear arsenal. As for other nuclear arsenals, this section briefly looks at smaller nuclear arsenals except for China's, which is discussed later.

THE U.K. AND FRANCE

The nuclear arsenals of the United Kingdom and France are well known and are not growing.

France has approximately 300 nuclear warheads. Most are SLBMs deployed on French navy vessels. The rest are ALCMs for delivery by fighter-bombers operated by the Strategic Air Forces and the Naval Nuclear Aviation Force. French navy fighters carrying nuclear-armed cruise missiles can be launched from the *Charles DeGaulle*, France's only aircraft carrier. French warheads reportedly have yields of 100 to 300 kilotons (kt). Each French SLBM reportedly carries four to six warheads, or multiple independently targetable reentry vehicles (MIRVs).[19]

The United Kingdom has an estimated 200 nuclear warheads, believed to be the "W76-1," a variant of the U.S. W76 warhead, with estimated yield of 90 kt. Because the British have significantly scaled back their nuclear arsenal and delivery vehicles since the end of the Cold War their nuclear arsenal consists entirely of SLBMs deployed on Trident submarines.

INDIA AND PAKISTAN

India and Pakistan's nuclear arsenals are assumed to be around 150 warheads each. Both nations are likely engaged in nuclear modernization efforts that are probably intended to increase the number and sophistication of their nuclear warheads.

India's nuclear arsenal is believed to be composed of plutonium-fueled fission and boosted-fission warheads. It reportedly consists of gravity bombs carried by fighters, land-based ballistic missiles of 12–40 kt and sea-based ballistic missiles of 12 kt or more.[20]

There is disagreement over the success of India's last nuclear tests in May 1998 that were believed intended to test boosted-fission or fusion warheads. Most experts believe these five tests failed but that India probably used data from them to perfect at least a boosted-fission design.

Pakistan reportedly has 140 to 150 nuclear weapons, believed to be fueled by enriched uranium. All are likely fission or boosted-fission weapons. Pakistan's arsenal is believed to consist of land-based ballistic missiles of 12–40 kt, ground- and air-launched cruise missiles of 12 kt, and sea-based cruise missiles of 12 kt.[21]

Pakistan matched India's May 1998 nuclear tests with five of its own and claimed it successfully tested a boosted-fission warhead. This claim has not been confirmed. India has probably continued its nuclear weapons research since 1998, possibly to perfect a thermonuclear warhead.

NORTH KOREA

North Korea, with a nuclear arsenal estimated at up to 100 warheads, may be the world's most dangerous nuclear state.

Figure 5: Comparison of Most Powerful Nuclear Tests by Country (Estimated explosive yields in kilotons)

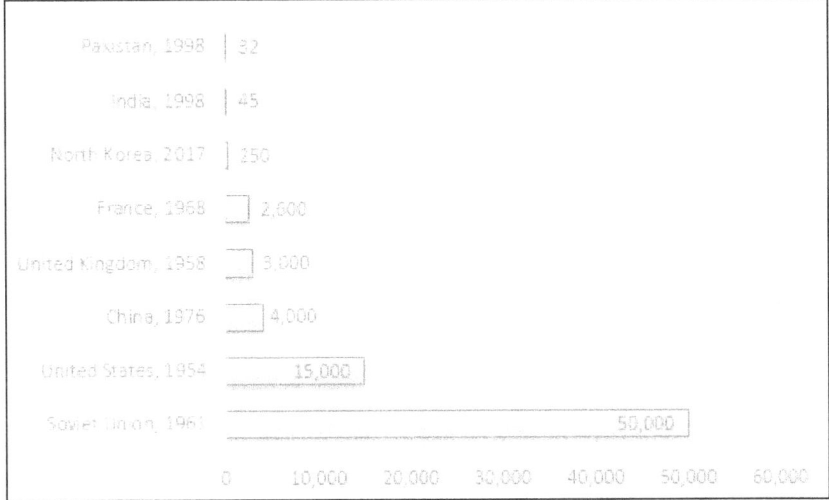

Center for Security Policy graphic.

Figure 6: Comparison of Estimated Yields of North Korean Nuclear Tests

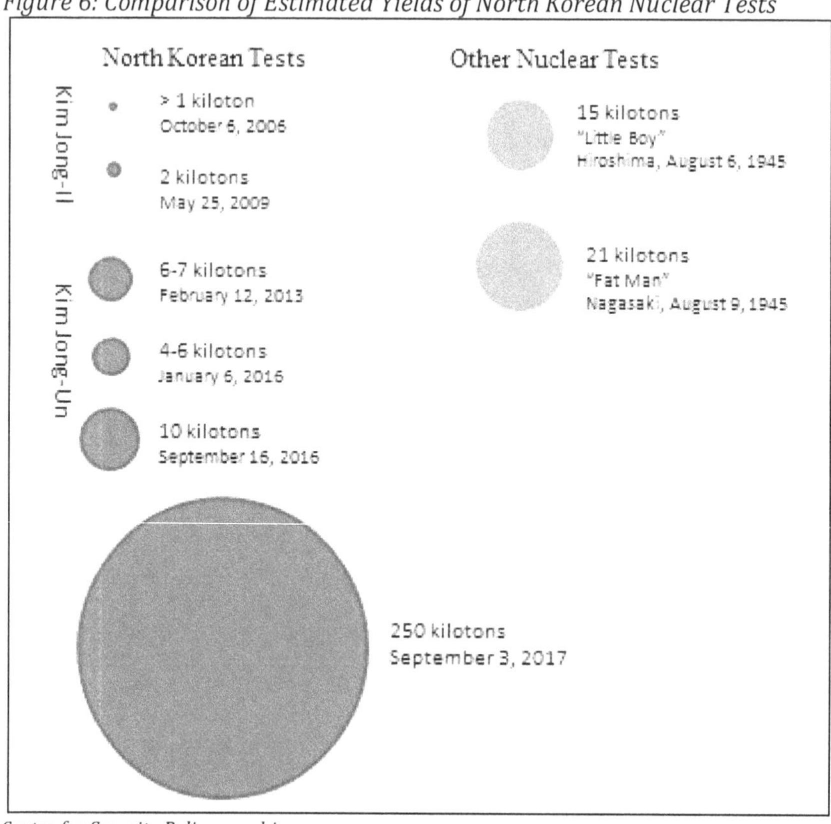

Center for Security Policy graphic.

The *New York Times* reported on March 13, 1993, that the CIA believed North Korea might have produced enough material to build a nuclear weapon.[22] President Clinton's CIA Director James Woolsey gave a similar warning in February 1993 that North Korea might be only months to a year away from producing its first atomic weapon. Deputy of State Lawrence Eagleburger testified to Congress on March 10, 1993, that he believed North Korea had already built a nuclear bomb.[23]

North Korea conducted six nuclear tests between 2006 and 2017. Each had increasing yields, growing from 0.5 kt in 2006 to an estimated 250 kt in 2017. It is known that most of North Korea's nuclear tests were plutonium-fueled. Some later tests may have been fueled by enriched uranium.

North Korea claims its 2017 nuclear test was a hydrogen bomb. Experts are divided on whether this was the case or if the device tested used boosted-fission. There was no doubt that the 2017 nuclear test represented a major and dangerous advance for North Korea's nuclear program.

North Korea has a large missile arsenal and tested missiles in 2017 with ICBM ranges. It also claims to be developing (or has developed) miniaturized nuclear warheads for its missiles and SLBMs.

North Korea suspended nuclear testing in 2018 in response to a diplomatic outreach from President Donald Trump. It also suspended its missile tests, but resumed short-range tests in mid-2019. There were fears in late 2019 that North Korea would resume tests of longer-range missiles, possibly ICBMs. However, such tests never occurred.

IRAN

Many experts believe that, despite its nuclear weapons research, Iran has not yet constructed a nuclear warhead. But given the country's close and formal collaborative relationship with North Korea in military matters, it is not out of the question that Iran now has nuclear warheads of some kind. Iran's nuclear weapons-related activities were supposed to have been suspended by the 2015 nuclear agreement with Iran, known as the Joint Comprehensive Program of Action, or JCPOA. The JCPOA, according to the Obama administration, was intended to keep Iran at least one year away from developing nuclear weapons. However, this agreement had very weak verification provisions and Iran has refused to allow International Atomic Energy Agency (IAEA) inspectors, whom it agreed to cooperate with to verify the agreement, access to military sites. There have been many credible reports of Iran cheating on its JCPOA obligations. President Trump withdrew from the JCPOA in 2018. Although Europe has tried to work with Iran to save the agreement, when this book went to print, Europe was close to admitting that the deal was dead. On January 14, 2020, France, Britain and Germany formally triggered the JCPOA dispute mechanism, a process that likely result in their exit from the agreement. President Trump has pledged his willingness to negotiate a better nuclear agreement with Iran that addresses the whole range of security threats Iran poses and is supported by regional states. So far, Iranian leaders have rejected President Trump's offer and its behavior worsened over since Mr. Trump's inauguration.

THE CONTEXT: AMERICAN NUCLEAR REDUCTIONS

Before we examine the Russian and Chinese nuclear arsenals, it should be understood that the United States has, more than any other country, markedly reduced its nuclear arsenal by tens of thousands of warheads from its peak, a reduction of near 90% when theater and battlefield nuclear weapons are considered. In congressional testimony, nuclear expert Madelyn Creedon noted that overall the U.S. nuclear inventory has declined from 31,255 warheads at the height of the Cold War to 3,800 today, including deployed and reserve nuclear warheads, an 88% reduction. These reductions have been in deployed "in the field" strategic and theater weapons, as well as in the "hedge" stockpile we have prudently maintained in case strategic deterrent requirements change.

HOW TO REVIEW U.S.-RUSSIA NUCLEAR INVENTORY

The United States maintains very close to the 1,550-warhead limit of the New START agreement, having an additional 200 theater or short-range warheads deployed with tactical aircraft in Europe. The United States also has a significant number of warheads—roughly 2,800—slated for complete dismantlement, that are not available for deployment.

Furthermore, there are zero strategic nuclear programs under development by the United States that do not fit within the terms of the New START treaty. On the other hand, Russia has six such strategic-capable nuclear systems under development or being deployed. Moscow claims that these systems are outside the parameters of the treaty. These warheads add appreciably to Russian "niche" nuclear capabilities, probably in the realm of hundreds of additional warheads in the near term.

Finally, while the popular bean-counting measures may include Russian theater or short-range nuclear systems, these are probably seriously undercounted and thus a further distorted view of the nuclear balance is often presented as fact.

Finally, what prompted the U.S. to suspend and then withdraw from its obligations under the INF Treaty in 2019 was not a Russian technical violation or an interpretive difference, but Russia's development, testing, and fielding of a ground-launched cruise missile system specifically banned by the INF Treaty. For those concerned that our suspension would cause Russia to develop these systems further, Russia's legal obligations under the INF Treaty proved no barrier to its pursuit and fielding of a banned system in the first place. To assert that Russia is reacting to our suspension is to ignore the reality of Russia's conduct under the INF Treaty since at least 2009. "Violations must have consequences," the White House said February 2019 in announcing its intent to withdraw. "Nearly 6 years of diplomacy and more than 30 meetings have failed to convince Russia to return to compliance with the INF Treaty. Enough is enough."[24]

NUCLEAR BALANCE BASICS

For Russia, its deployed "in the field" strategic long-range nuclear warheads (including bomber weapons) are assumed to number, based in part on decade-old data, roughly 2,300. The quantity may be considerably higher, even counting just those systems that come under the New START treaty of 2010. Figure 7 illustrates U.S. and Russian commitments under New START.

Figure 7: U.S. and Russian Long-range Nuclear Forces Under New START

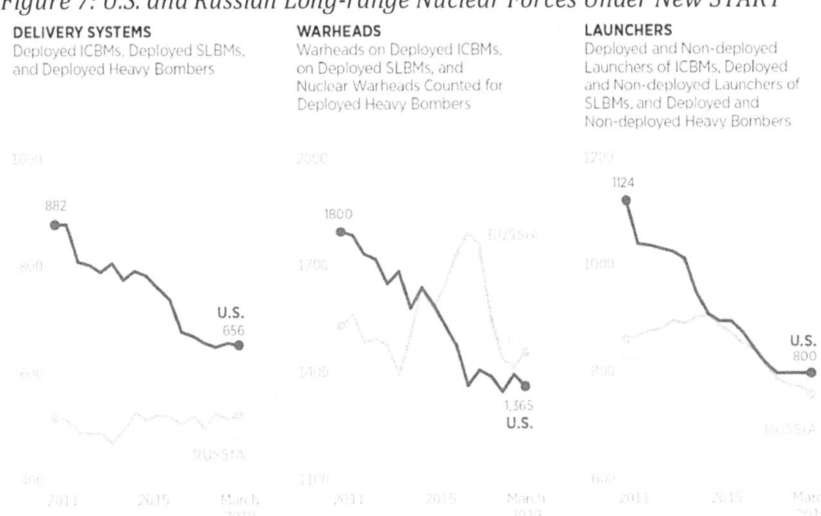

Heritage Foundation Chart used with permission.

Given the six major strategic weapons systems the Russians are now building that fall outside the 2010 New START framework, plus the current strategic force of 2,300 warheads, plus theater or short-range nuclear weapons, **Russia could have at least three times the number of deployed weapons than are officially allowed by the New START treaty.** In addition, China's nuclear arsenal is of an unknown size, is believed to be growing, and is not subject to any nuclear arms control agreement.

Eight points need to be kept in mind when comparing Russian and Chinese nuclear weapons to U.S. nuclear forces.

First, the Russian nuclear arsenal is made up of strategic or long-range platforms that carry nuclear weapons. Moreover, there are short-range and what are often described as theater nuclear weapons that run the gamut from nuclear land mines and artillery shells to lower-yield gravity bombs and rocket and short-range missile warheads.

Second, some key elements of the Russian strategic arsenal are bound by the 2010 New START arms control agreement, but many new strategic systems are not captured by the agreement and thus have to be considered when projecting what the Russian nuclear threat might look like in the future.

Third, Russian theater or tactical nuclear weapons are not covered by any arms control agreement. For the past three decades, the U.S. intelligence community has estimated Russian theater nuclear forces at between 2,000 and 5,000 warheads, with a recent National Intelligence Estimate centered on 2,000.

The problem with such theater systems is that they are small, difficult to verify using national technical means—satellites, primarily— and are easy to hide. By contrast, the U.S. has 500 nuclear gravity bombs, of which 300 are in reserve storage. The remaining 200 are deployed aboard nuclear-capable fighter aircraft in several NATO-allied nations.

Russia has claimed that it has reduced its tactical nuclear weapons by 70%. Using open literature sources, such a reduction still gives Russia a remaining nuclear force considerably above 2,000 warheads.

Fourth, many nuclear warheads in the U.S. arsenal are scheduled for dismantlement and disposal, meaning that they are not available for deploying into the deterrent force, but this fact is often ignored in various assessments of the nuclear balance.

Fifth, it is also usually assumed that because Russian strategic nuclear forces deployed or in the field are contained within the parameters of the New START treaty, they thus do not exceed 1,550 warheads, except bomber warheads that have their own special counting rules.

But insofar as fast flyers are concerned—ICBMs and SLBMs—it is assumed the Russian systems are no more than 700 strategic nuclear delivery vehicles (SNDVs) and 1,490 warheads. This assumption is largely based on a 2009 Russian declaration submitted under START I rules, and since then on only partial information provided by Russia but that remains classified.

Most importantly, New START verification measures are weaker than those originally adopted under START I. Furthermore, as Michaela Dodge explained in a Heritage Foundation paper, "the US negotiated away telemetry provisions that would allow us to get an insight into how many warheads can be carried by Russian missiles. Moreover, warheads in maintenance facilities and systems away from a base are off-limits to inspectors, further diminishing our understanding of the composition of Russia's nuclear forces. Inexplicably, the New START treaty also allows concealment activities on ICBM bases."[25]

Proponents of New START argue that the treaty allows the United States to count the actual overall number of deployed Russian warheads. This argument is misleading because the structure of New START does not give the United States the ability to count Russia's warheads with much confidence.

First, bombers are counted as one warhead regardless of how many warheads they actually carry.

Second, as Dodge explains, "warheads in maintenance facilities or on systems away from a base at the time of inspection as well as the mobile launchers and warheads within them are off-limits to inspectors, providing a loophole to deploy more warheads than declared under New START."[26]

Third, notes Dodge, "New START does not contain limits on a maximum warhead number deployed per missile and does not set throw-weight limitations and launch-weight limitations. Russia is also developing and deploying new nuclear warheads and launchers, some not constrained by New START."

If these new warheads are smaller than warheads that Russia has deployed in the past, Russia can deploy many more of them above New START levels with no appreciable risk of being caught during an inspection.

Fourth, as Dodge explains, "for all intents and purposes, Russia's telemetry regime is all but eliminated for verification purposes since Russia decides which data it will share. Telemetry helps the United States understand one of the key characteristics of a ballistic missile: its throw weight, which helps to determine how many warheads a missile can carry. It can also show when a missile releases a re-entry vehicle (RV)."

In New START, Russia rejected what Dodge notes was the more effective first Strategic Arms Reduction Treaty "look alike, count alike" approach and type rules. Under the old regime, each missile was attributed several warheads it could carry regardless of how many warheads an inspector saw on it during an onsite inspection. The Russians misled the United States about capabilities of their missiles, but nevertheless this approach allowed the United States to better understand a baseline capability of Russia's missile forces. Taken together, the limitations of New START mean that even if an inspector finds a missile deploying more RVs than the United States thinks Russia can deploy, it does not say much about how many RVs other missiles of the same type in the Russian arsenal carry. Also, it does not provide information about an RV capacity of missiles in Russia's arsenal, making it very difficult to charge the Russians with a violation of New START. Even the unique identifiers do not add much to the verification regime per se; since they can be decided upon by each of the parties, it is difficult, if not impossible, to determine whether they have been tampered with.

Sixth, it is also assumed that the reserve stockpiles of the U.S. and Russia are somehow comparable. However, the American reserve hedge is critical because the U.S. has through neglect given up the ability to build new nuclear warheads, a capability the Trump administration is seeking to reestablish.

Russia, on the other hand, can build warheads as fast as a beer festival in Hamburg can turn out sausage and thus doesn't need a large hedged stockpile. And in fact, a lot of the Russian "stockpile" of warheads hides the extent to which the Russian "in the field" or "deployed" force of warheads may be considerably above the official "assumed" New START level. The reason is because individual missile warhead loadings are not constrained in the treaty but are assumed to have been reduced across the Russian missile forces to fit within the treaty allowance.

There is also an unwritten rule within the intelligence community that since 1972, when the first SALT nuclear arms treaty was signed between the Soviet Union and the United States, violations of such agreements, however accurately determined, were to be dealt with at a political level, by the policy experts in the White House rather than the intelligence community.

Thus, the accountability of nuclear weapons is not an intelligence matter, but a political one. When former President Clinton was asked about certifying violations of arms agreements by our adversaries, he noted he would rather not know about such violations because once made public, there would be Congressional and other demands to take compensatory action. Thus, the announcement of and reaction to arms treaty violations is a highly charged political problem. The result is we are loath to call out Russia for its treaty violations and, even if we do, the only "remedy" we have is to publicize the violation and either shame Moscow into compliance, or allow the Kremlin to manipulate our political system to gain its desired result.

Seventh, the Chinese nuclear arsenal is also problematic. Unlike the Russian media and official spokesmen, the Chinese reveal almost nothing about their nuclear arsenal and nuclear policy. Furthermore, all Chinese nuclear weapons go free in the sense that there is no arms control agreement of any kind that limits the deployment of any Chinese nuclear system.

And the argument over the relative size of the Chinese nuclear arsenal is largely an argument among foreign observers of Chinese policy and military action, as there are no public sources of official data inside China on Chinese nuclear missiles, submarines, bombers, or warheads.

The Chinese know this and thus engage in a kabuki dance of obfuscation and denial that their nuclear arsenal is anything but very small and their nuclear strategy anything but largely defensive and pacifist.

Eighth, apart from satellite imagery and whatever human intelligence we can secure, the Chinese nuclear arsenal and its companion strategy is largely opaque. The range of estimates of its arsenal vary from somewhat fewer than 300 warheads to as many as 1,800 to 3,000, which both American and Russian specialists have put forward. This estimated difference of as much as 1,000% is destabilizing and makes U.S. defense planning impossible.

One key point of departure of this analysis is my willingness to carefully examine the assumption that China's low level of plutonium and nuclear fuel capability makes it a foregone conclusion that China's nuclear force structure is quite low when we are in fact only considering the low end of the estimates of the current Chinese stockpile. Here the assumption is that China has a limited nuclear force because its nuclear-weapons-grade fuel production capacity is limited, and its fuel capacity is obviously limited because it only has a small nuclear arsenal deployed. This circular logic is then added to a further assumption that because China has a policy of targeting only American cities with very large, megaton-class warheads, a deployment of such large nuclear warheads is obviously constrained by China's limited nuclear warhead fuel production capability.

RUSSIAN NUCLEAR BEANS

As I have explained, the usual inventory estimates of the world's nuclear arsenals are often bean-counting exercises that say nothing of the capability of the force to expand quickly, the purpose of the force, the structure of the force, and the relationship of the force to a country's strategic objectives.

Russian President Putin says that he regards nuclear modernization as the nation's highest priority and is focused on providing Russia with a "guaranteed nuclear deterrent." In April 2000, soon after taking power, Putin declared that in a crisis or conventional conflict, Russia would reserve the right to use nuclear weapons first, in small numbers or in limited strikes, but nonetheless first. And over the next two decades, he affirmed the building and testing of such theater nuclear systems as well as declaring that sometime in the very near future, Russia will have fully built and deployed such systems. Meanwhile, Russia produced and deployed new generations of ICBMs, ballistic missile submarines and SLBMs, maneuverable ballistic missiles and/or warheads, and hypersonic missiles against which the U.S. has no defense.

In addition, during its military operation against Crimea, Russia raised the alert level of its nuclear forces and issued veiled nuclear threats to ensure the West did not intervene. In July 2017, Putin signed a new naval doctrine that stated, "under conditions of escalation of a military conflict, demonstration of readiness and determination to use force, including the use of nonstrategic nuclear weapons, is an effective deterrent factor."[27] Later, in his annual state-of-the-nation address on February 20, 2019, Putin revived a Soviet policy of the early 1980s by saying that if Washington deployed intermediate-range missiles in Europe to counter what Russia had put in place, Moscow would target the countries hosting the U.S. weapons.

This nuclear strategy is designed to get the United States to stand down in the face of Russian aggression. That challenge, explained Under Secretary of Defense John Rood in July 2019, is the Russian doctrine that seems to believe that at a "certain level they could use small nuclear weapons against the United States and our allies and not face a similar response."[28]

For example, should Russia invade one of the NATO-member Baltic republics, Putin is counting on NATO failing to invoke the alliance's cornerstone Article 5 for mutual defense and being unwilling to come to the defense of a NATO ally. That failure would defeat the entire purpose of NATO, likely leading to the complete collapse of the trans-Atlantic alliance, and with it, America's leadership of the free world. Russia could then declare to the countries of Europe, now unable to rely upon the U.S. for its security, that it is time they make their own security deals with Russia in what the Soviets once called a "common European home."

In this context, the Russian nuclear arsenal takes on a different color than the common "arms control" disarmament renditions by the Stockholm International Peace Research Institute or the Federation of American Scientists. As former House Armed Services Committee Chairman and Secretary of Defense Les Aspin once told this writer, "Counting the nuclear beans is all well and good, but tell me what the bad guys are going to do with the beans that is not good for the United States."

Michaela Dodge's Heritage Foundation essay on the subject explains exactly what "no good" the Russians are up to. She writes, "Russia's provocative steps suggest that it mistakenly believes that it can exploit gaps at the lower levels of the escalatory ladder and control escalation of a nuclear conflict to achieve its objectives without risking a strategic nuclear exchange with the United States, even as it publicly denies such is the case."[29]

Thus, the question of Russia's tactical nuclear capabilities is not just academic. Writes Dodge: "If Russia believes it can exploit gaps on the lower levels of the so-called escalatory ladder, it is more likely to miscalculate in a conflict. It could also be more likely to pursue aggressive foreign policies involving conventional weapons."

In that overall context of the Russian nuclear doctrine, the Russian nuclear inventory can be better appreciated and analyzed.

The New START treaty allows each side 700 strategic nuclear delivery vehicles (SNDVs), otherwise known as operational strategic missiles and bombers. Both sides can have 100 additional SNDVs in reserve above the 700.

In reality, while the U.S. reduced its SNDVs to meet the treaty parameters, the Russians built up. Russia increased its delivery vehicles from 521 to 524, while the U.S. cut delivery vehicles from 882 to 656. As for warheads, the U.S. dropped from 1,800 to 1,365, while Russia claims it went from 1,537 to 1,461 on the day New START was officially meant to be implemented.

The warhead levels for the New START treaty are 1,550 for each side. But this number of warheads is misleading. Actually, each side pledged by 2018 to reach no more than 1,490 SLBM and ICBM warheads, with 60 additional bombers, each of which could have multiple gravity bombs or cruise missiles but would only count for purposes of the treaty as one warhead per bomber, up to 60 such airplanes.

Now before we list the missiles the Russians have deployed—put into the field—we must explain the verification rules adopted under New START. In the first arms reduction treaty for strategic weapons, START I, it was assumed that each missile carried the maximum number of warheads that had been tested on that class of missile. That was the number of warheads to be inferred by the deployment of a certain number of ICBMs and SLBMs.

For New START, however, the disarmament advocates wanted to count the exact number of warheads and adopt a new counting rule. So, ten times a year, the U.S. can ask with 24-hour notice to inspect one of the 478 missiles in the Russian arsenal. American inspectors can go to a Russian military base, be shown a list of missiles deployed at that base, and ask to inspect the missile of choice, whether in a silo or mounted on a truck. The Russians can then direct the American inspectors to the right missile. The inspectors can see the missile has only two, four, or six warheads, whatever was listed in the declaration, and can then can proceed to tell the American people that the United States officially knows that a Russian SS-18 or SS-24 or SS-25 ICBM at a certain base has a certain number of warheads.

But here is the problem. That is all we can tell the American people. As Senator Kit Bond told the Senate in 2010, the procedures adopted under the New START treaty "do not permit adequate verification activities needed to make sure the Russians aren't cheating." As a result, the Senator explained, "I cannot in good conscience support the treaty."[30]

All the United States can do is say that out of the nearly 500 Russian missiles, when we saw the missiles on the day of inspection, we may know that ten missiles had "x" number of warheads—unless, of course, the warheads are camouflaged by hard covers.

Now the assumption many observers as well as analysts of the nuclear balance make is that all missiles in a particular category are only loaded with warheads as indicated in a declared classified inventory by Russia that does not exceed 1,490. After all, the U.S. inspectors might get lucky and inspect a missile that has warhead loadings exceeding the declaration if in fact Russia is cheating.

However, as Dodge explains, "the New START's verification regime is limited at best and, at worst, tends to provide U.S. politicians and policymakers with a false sense of security. The issues with New START's verification provisions are so severe that the New START Working Group, consisting of analysts from The Heritage Foundation and other organizations, called it 'Potemkin village verification.'"[31]

Dodge continues: "The reality is that not a single inspection allowed under New START is capable of proving a violation of New START. At the time the treaty was submitted to the Senate's advice-and-consent process, the Obama Administration argued that the U.S. no longer needs as much verification as before."

However, is that enough verification in a deal that cannot rely on trust? Unfortunately, one of Senator Bond's concerns was that every missile in the Russian inventory can be loaded with as many warheads as the Russians are physically able to deploy. So, inspecting one or ten missiles a year is verification of only that missile at the time of inspection, nothing more and nothing less.

But, say treaty supporters, the Russians are meant to reduce their warhead loadings to comply with the 2010 treaty, and official assessments from the State Department, for example, claim the Russians are complying.

This is based on the State Department's assumption that deployed Russian missiles on trucks, in silos, and on submarines would easily carry

2,670 warheads, says one longtime arms control annual assessment, not the lower number required by the treaty.

These 2,670 warheads are deployed aboard 478 Russian missiles and 68 bombers, ranging from 318 ICBMs on six different ICBM systems to 720 warheads on 10 submarines carrying 160 missiles of three different types, plus 68 bombers of three types—Bear 6, Bear 16, and Blackjack—carrying 786 warheads.

Here is the big unknown: It is assumed that Russia has downloaded its 2,670 warheads—considered the normal, day-to-day deployed capable level of weapons, including bombers not on alert and submarines in port undergoing a refit or overhaul—to the treaty-compliant 2,276 level, which would consist of 1,490 missile warheads and roughly 786 bomber weapons.

Now, if the Russians wanted to place on each missile and bomber the maximum number of warheads technically possible, and add in the estimated minimum of 1,800–2,000 warheads they have for theater or shorter-range requirements, then they could deploy in the near term 4,700 strategic and theater warheads on a day-to-day basis.

But as noted earlier, the Russians also have six new nuclear "superweapons," at least four of which are not restricted by the New START treaty, while two are constrained.

David Trachtenberg, a former Trump administration deputy assistant secretary of defense, explained to Congress in March 2019:

In March 2018, only a month after the United States and Russia reached the limits on strategic systems established under the New START Treaty, President Vladimir Putin announced that Russia is actively testing five new nuclear weapons capabilities, which include: 1) an intercontinental-range, nuclear armed hypersonic glide vehicle; 2) a maneuverable, nuclear armed air-launched ballistic missile; 3) a long-range, nuclear-powered cruise missile; 4) a nuclear-powered, nuclear-armed underwater unmanned vehicle; and 5) a new heavy intercontinental range ballistic missile, called the SARMAT. President Putin, during this same speech, also announced that Russia developed new laser weapons systems "that have been supplied to the troops since last year."[32]

Some of these systems are relatively close to being operational, with the RS-28 Sarmat's (up to 24 warheads) initial operational capability being 2021, the year New START is currently set to expire.

According to national security expert Mark Schneider, who contributed a chapter to this book, the Tsirkon hypersonic missile was added in 2019 to be fully deployed as the Sarmat goes on duty. As for the nuclear-powered cruise missile and the Poseidon drone submarine, initial operations will soon follow. The Avangard hypersonic boost glide vehicle was scheduled for deployment in 2019. To avoid falling under New START limitations, says Schneider, Moscow may assert the Sarmat missile version carrying the Avangard payload is not the same missile as the Sarmat that carries the 24 warheads.

An excellent 2015 study by James R. Howe concluded that Russia had the potential to deploy 2,664–5,890 nuclear warheads on its planned strategic ballistic missile force. In another analysis published in September 2019, he says Russia will have between "2,976 WHs [warheads], and a maximum of 6,670 WHs" plus over 800 bomber weapons. He notes that "the 2022 [Russian] strategic nuclear force's (SNFs) war-head (WH) levels will likely significantly exceed New START levels based on planned WH loadings."

To further understand the dimensions of the Russian nuclear arsenal, three additional points need to be understood. First, the Russian nuclear arsenal likely will greatly outpace America's even if the U.S. meets the 2018 Nuclear Posture Review's goal of producing 80 nuclear pits per year. (A pit is the trigger for detonating a thermonuclear weapon, or hydrogen bomb. It is a hollow shell of plutonium and other materials surrounded by chemical explosives.) The U.S. is racing to produce pits to extend the life of older nuclear weapons because of uncertainty about the useful life of pits, which could be as little as 45 years.[33] In some estimates, the Russians will have as high as a 100 to 1 advantage if U.S. pit production gets only to the 30 per year called for by the House Armed Services Committee. In December 2019, Congress approved the Trump administration's request for funding in the 2020 National Defense Authorization Act to resume production of plutonium pits. (See Chapter 10).

Second, Moscow can add warheads to missiles by making the current warheads smaller and thus uploading missiles to the maximum technical level, which in most circumstances for the Russians, exceeds the missiles' assumed current loadings.

Third, the Russians see nuclear weapons as coercive instruments of statecraft, where their aggression and use of military force is to be used to grab territory and geostrategic advantage and not simply as a deterrent to respond to aggression by another state.

CHINA'S NUCLEAR INVENTORY

Not a single Chinese nuclear warhead is controlled by a nuclear arms treaty. The current extent and projected future size of China's nuclear arsenal remain an exquisite puzzle.

The most common minimalist view of China's nuclear forces assumes 187 land-based missiles, 48 sea-based missiles, and 20 aircraft, with a total of 290 warheads, reflecting a view that most of China's nuclear forces have only one warhead per missile, while some have two. A refreshing exception to this "rule" has been Defense Intelligence Agency estimates that project a Chinese nuclear arsenal in 2029 from 600 to 800 deployed long-range strategic warheads. These numbers are more consistent with the admittedly sparse information publicly available today on the Chinese nuclear arsenal than they are with the usual minimalist estimates of China's nuclear forces that have dominated the limited discussion of such forces for the past few decades.

Based on Defense Intelligence Agency projections, it could be that China deploys 398 missiles and bombers carrying 606 warheads, reflecting growth in warheads per missile of up to four to six in limited cases. Russian intelligence sources, as well as the former chief of staff of the Russian Strategic Rocket Forces General Victor Esin, conclude that China has 2,000 theater-range missiles, many of which are dual-use—both conventional and nuclear. Thus, it is not a stretch to conclude that China's warhead holdings may exceed 1,000 in the near term and reach, according to Rick Fisher, a projected 2,200 in 2029.[34]

This analysis concludes that the common assumptions of the West underlying the lower Chinese numbers are as dubious as those historically adopted with respect to Russia. Many experts believe that that because Chinese warheads are not mated with missiles or bomber platforms, they are only for retaliatory purposes. This is hardly true if the Chinese are building strategic submarines—unless Chinese officials plan to send their troops to sea and pretend to be in a deterrent role as their associated warheads are left on the mainland.

It is also further assumed[35] that China's minimalist and declared "no first use" nuclear strategy is predicated[36] on a retaliatory deterrent policy of just threatening to blow up American cities (a counter-value strategy), not a policy of holding at risk U.S. military assets (a counter-force strategy), including our nuclear weapons capabilities.

As such, it had been assumed[37] that Chinese leaders do not have ambitions to build a bigger and more sophisticated nuclear arsenal than a counterforce strategy supposedly would require. Such an assumption supposes that the simple reiteration of Chinese government propaganda about Beijing's nuclear arsenal is perfectly acceptable as the intelligence and policy basis for ongoing American professional assessments.

Missing is a comparison of possible Chinese nuclear deployments not just revealed by American and allied national technical means, but by any analysis that even begins to question the widespread acceptance of a minimalist interpretation of Chinese nuclear intentions and projected capabilities.

China continues its expansive military modernization and is focused on establishing regional dominance and expanding its ability to coerce U.S. allies and partners. Consistent with a military strategy that stresses "optimization of its nuclear force structure," China is modernizing and rapidly expanding its already considerable nuclear forces, with little to no transparency regarding the scope and scale of its nuclear modernization program. China is the only permanent United Nations Security Council member country that has not announced publicly the size of its nuclear arsenal. Beijing has also rebuffed multiple U.S. attempts to engage in a meaningful bilateral dialogue on nuclear posture and risk reduction issues.

China is developing a new generation of mobile missiles, with warheads consisting of MIRVs and penetration aids. In particular, Beijing has developed an advanced ballistic missile submarine armed with new SLBMs. In a huge military parade in 2019, on the 70th anniversary of Mao Tse-tung's proclamation of Communist China, the regime unveiled a new road-mobile strategic ICBM, the Dongfeng-41 (DF-41), which bears physical resemblance to Russia's Topol-M and reportedly carries at least 10 nuclear warheads.

China has also announced development of a new nuclear-capable strategic bomber, indicating its intent to develop a nuclear triad, and has deployed a nuclear-capable precision-guided DF-26 IRBM capable of attacking land and naval targets. China also tested a hypersonic glide vehicle in 2014.

China's nuclear forces include a mix of strategic-range systems capable of striking the American homeland and any other point on earth as well as theater-range forces capable of threatening allies, U.S. bases, and forces in the region.

The usual bean counters, having no official information from China, adopt through inertia the same minimalist assumptions used other bean counters, coming up with a small Chinese nuclear arsenal of around 280 warheads and rejecting any alternative assessment of China's current or projected nuclear arsenal. Of still greater concern are China's funding and infiltration of American academic institutions to influence the perceptions of American intelligence officers, coupled with aggressive—

and sometimes successful—attempts to co-opt and recruit U.S. military and intelligence officers and analysts.

Admiral David Kriete, the Deputy Commander of the U.S. Strategic Command, explained, "China is and has been for the last couple of decades on a very clear trajectory where they're increasing the numbers of nuclear weapons that they field, they're increasing the number of and diversity of the delivery systems," and "contrary to common assumptions, [will be] expanding its nuclear weapons production capabilities."[38]

Kriete says that China's new forces include new mobile land-based missiles, including the DF-41. Bill Gertz also reports that China is nearing deployment of a hypersonic glide vehicle—a maneuvering ultra-high-speed missile that can defeat missile defenses.

Another official, Rear Admiral Michael Brookes, director of intelligence for the Pacific Command, said in August 2019 that China's nuclear forces modernization is a concern, explaining that in the last decade China has doubled its nuclear force and plans to double it again in the next decade, even as the United States has been reducing its nuclear arsenal during that same period of time by nearly 70% through both the 2002 Moscow and 2010 New START strategic arms agreements.[39]

In a May 2019 speech, Lieutenant General Robert P. Ashley, Director of the Defense Intelligence Agency, called China's recent nuclear modernization "the most rapid expansion and diversification of its nuclear arsenal in China's history." One key aspect is the 3,000 miles of tunnels built by the Chinese to hide their ballistic missiles, but described by some as simply a major public works program of no military significance. On the other hand, when the U.S. determined that the cost of the construction if done by the West would be north of $60 billion, it is obvious that a nation would not spend that kind of money protecting just a small inventory of nuclear missiles and warheads, with missiles spaced some 15 miles apart.

Tong Zhao, an analyst for the Carnegie-Tsinghua Center for Global Policy in Beijing, argued in a March 2019 article that without the extension of New START, China would not trust the announced levels of nuclear weapons held by the United States and would develop exaggerated threat perceptions, leading to a growing Chinese nuclear arsenal. Zhao did admit that China's nuclear arsenal was already expanding and being modernized.[40]

Zhao further explained that arms control agreements provide certainty about the capabilities of the nuclear parties, without which they are only uncertain rules and the "nuclear communities would stop talking."

Unsaid by Zhao was an obviously unfortunate failure to appreciate the full implications of his remarks: China refuses to be part of any arms control agreement that gives anyone certainty about Beijing's nuclear arsenal. But China demands such certainty from the United States, a double standard that the Trump administration's proposal for China's entrance into arms control is meant to address. However, the arms control community sides with the Chinese Communist Party as does the echo chamber of the U.S. national media such as CNN, confirming the central thesis of this essay that the policy-driven nuclear inventory books are often cooked and the nuclear narrative rigged. As we are faced with increasing nuclear dangers, an unflinching review of the world's nuclear inventories is more necessary than ever.

CONCLUSION

Contrary to popular belief, the United States and Russia, while possessing together over half of all the nuclear warheads deployed or stockpiled worldwide, do not have arsenals that are roughly equal in size.

Furthermore, not only is Russia now deploying and not only can it purposely deploy into the future a force upwards of 500% of the total U.S. deployed or in-the-field warheads, it is now in possession of nuclear forces some four times the level of U.S. forces, due to both the deployment of long-range strategic forces and medium- or theater-range missiles and warheads. In addition, the U.S. cannot now build new warheads although the current proposed budget calls for it to regain such a capability over the next decade.

Not only that, but China has deployed a nuclear force that is being rapidly expanded to the 600–700 warhead level and may be significantly higher depending upon the warheads one assumes are deployed on China's dual-use medium-range missiles.

Finally, the significance of this assessment is that both Russia and China see nuclear weapons as very significant tools of political coercion and blackmail. In particular, most reckless has been Russia adopting some two decades ago a policy of using nuclear weapons early in a crisis or conflict to force the United States and its allies to surrender, a policy now being gradually adopted by China as well.

Added to proliferation issues in Iran and North Korea, the nuclear landscape is vastly different than that portrayed by the idealistic proponents of nuclear warhead elimination, especially with respect to the necessity for and stabilizing nature of the United States nuclear deterrent modernization effort now being undertaken.

Nuclear Arms Control and U.S. Security Interests

By Ambassadors Robert Joseph and Eric Edelman

Editor's Note: This article was originally published by National Review Online with the title "New Directions in Arms Control." It has been expanded and updated for this publication.

With the end of the INF treaty, attention has shifted to the question of whether to extend the New START treaty, soon be the only remaining agreement limiting the size of the U.S. and Russian nuclear arsenals. Under its terms, New START will expire in February 2021 unless both parties agree to an extension of up to five years. Advocates—in the arms-control community, in Congress, and reportedly some in the Trump administration—argue that there is an urgent need to endorse extension now. Their principal argument is that if New START expires, the entire fabric of the Cold War arms-control structure crafted with the Soviet Union will unravel and ignite a nuclear arms race. The question of extending New START, however, is far more complex and must be assessed considering fundamental changes in the geostrategic environment since the treaty was negotiated a decade ago.

The complexities of that new environment were on full view when U.S. and Russian officials met in Geneva on July 17, 2019. At the meeting, the U.S. reportedly presented a vision for a 21st-century arms control model that would include a possible agreement broader than New START, a treaty negotiated 20 years after the fall of the wall but based on the bilateral Cold War pattern of strategic arms control agreements. Given China's emergence as a global power, accompanied by the continued expansion of its nuclear arsenal, the U.S. made its position clear: any future treaty limiting U.S. nuclear forces cannot be tied only to Russia but must include China. For its part, Russia appears to have returned to its longstanding demand that any agreement must cover not only offensive strategic arms, but also set limits on missile defenses, a position that the U.S. has consistently rejected since Reagan refused to abandon the Strategic Defense Initiative when he met Gorbachev at Reykjavik in 1985. The Trump administration's 2019 Missile Defense Review states, "the United States will not accept any limitation or constraint on the development or deployment of missile defense capabilities needed to protect the homeland against rogue missile threats." Understanding the background of the positions of parties involved is essential to understanding the potential for a future arms control treaty.

It is important to acknowledge the logic of the Trump administration's decision to withdraw from the INF treaty. Here the facts are clear. Russian violations of the treaty—followed by years of failed diplomatic efforts by both the Obama and Trump administrations to bring Russia back into compliance—left withdrawal as the only viable option. It makes no sense to maintain an agreement that bans two countries from a particular military capability if only one is abiding by the terms and the other is cheating, all while China, North Korea, and Iran are developing their own formidable arsenals of intermediate-range missiles. Failure to impose costs on Russia for its ongoing violations would undercut prospects for future meaningful arms control by establishing that there are no consequences for breaching the central provisions of agreements.

Moreover, the security situation in Europe and Asia has changed considerably with Russian deployments of modern INF capabilities and China's large-scale buildup of dual-capable mobile missiles (i.e., those that can carry either a nuclear or a conventional payload). As the National Defense Strategy suggests, the U.S. deterrent in both regions has deteriorated significantly over the past decade. In the absence of countervailing U.S. military capabilities, the prospects for deterrence failure and the likelihood that our adversaries will test U.S. resolve by using their capabilities to intimidate and coerce U.S. allies increase dramatically. While most, if not all, of the needed capabilities are likely to be conventional rather than nuclear, these deployments would have been precluded by remaining in the INF Treaty.

It is also important to revisit the fundamental flaws of New START. In 2010, both authors testified against ratification, highlighting the treaty's shortcomings and providing our prediction, now proven accurate, that U.S. forces would go down and Russia would build up under the agreement. This was consistent with longstanding Soviet tactics that consistently used arms control to limit U.S. nuclear forces in a manner intended to gain unilateral advantages. We also emphasized the failure to limit theater nuclear forces, based on the fiction that nuclear attacks employing weapons with ranges less than 5,500 kilometers (3,400 miles) would not be strategic. For those who cared about whether agreements actually reduced the number of nuclear weapons on each side, we pointed out that the new bomber-counting rule contained in the fine print of New START allowed the deployment of more strategic warheads than the nominal 1,550 treaty limit since it counted each bomber as one without regard to the actual weapons load. We also noted that Russia would likely deploy offensive strategic forces not explicitly restricted by the agreement, which it has now done. Finally, we warned that the treaty, in principle and practice, seemed to accept at least some limits on missile defenses and conventional, prompt global-strike capabilities.

While these flaws were likely fully understood by the U.S. negotiators, the view of the Obama administration, reflected in its 2010 Nuclear Posture Review, was that preventing nuclear proliferation was the overriding priority. The administration asserted that preventing proliferation would be advanced by leading through example, taking steps toward a nuclear-free world, including measures that amounted to unilateral disarmament. There has never been any empirical evidence to support this proposition, as a recent study by Georgetown Professor Matthew Kroenig has persuasively demonstrated. The administration's view of Russia was that while it could be difficult to deal with, it was more of a partner than a threat that needed to be deterred. This benign view of Russia would change only with Moscow's military intervention in Ukraine and the annexation of Crimea. Putin's support for Assad in Syria illustrated his determination to challenge the U.S. at every opportunity.

Looking forward, any new negotiations with Russia must consider the realities of today's security setting. These include the following:

- With U.S. loss of technical, policy, and operational competence in nuclear weapons, which is only now beginning to be recovered, Russia has likely succeeded in its determined drive to achieve superiority in nuclear forces at both the theater and the strategic level. Moscow has for years invested heavily in its nuclear modernization program, developing and now deploying new mobile and heavy ICBMs, new submarine platforms and ballistic missiles, and an array of novel weapons, from longer-range underwater drones with megaton yields to air- and ground-launched cruise missiles based on new technologies to a family of hypersonic weapons. Russia claims many of these weapons are not covered under New START, which demonstrates either another fundamental flaw of the treaty or the intention of Moscow to cheat on yet another arms-control agreement—or both.

- Russia has moved to a military doctrine that emphasizes the centrality of nuclear weapons at all levels of conflict, including nuclear threats in peacetime to deter the U.S. and coerce our allies, and the use of theater nuclear weapons to prevail in conventional conflicts.

- While Russia today has active production lines for a wide range of platforms and new warheads, the U.S. is only slowly moving forward to modernize its nuclear triad with uncertain funding and political impediments. Those who fear an arms race without New START ignore the race that started more than a decade ago, when Russia began aggressively enlarging and modernizing its nuclear forces (even with New START in place) while the U.S. largely stood still.

According to the Director of the Defense Intelligence Agency, Russia's nuclear buildup appears to be accompanied by low-yield testing inconsistent with the zero-yield standard adopted by the United States as a signatory to the Comprehensive Test Ban Treaty. While the treaty fails to define what it purports to prohibit, Russian low-yield tests—used to develop new theater nuclear weapons and to manage the existing stockpile—would be clearly inconsistent with the intent of the treaty, and therefore yet another violation of a central arms control commitment.

Given that Russia today is a clear threat to the U.S. and our allies, and given the detrimental changes in the nuclear balance, any future arms-control negotiations must include all nuclear-weapons types. The Senate's 2010 ratification of New START made it clear that any future agreement with Russia must consider the huge disparity in theater capabilities. As Russia has expanded its nuclear forces at all ranges and in all theaters, making the distinction between strategic and nonstrategic weapons increasingly meaningless, this Senate-imposed condition has become even more important to incorporate into our arms control posture. This is especially the case for assuring U.S. allies and deterring Russia in Europe, where Russia reportedly holds a 10-to-1 advantage in theater systems.

China's nuclear forces must also be included in any future negotiations. Beijing and Moscow have greatly expanded their defense relationships to include larger-scale military exercises and, most recently, joint air patrols. In the nuclear area, China has been modernizing and expanding its arsenal for the past decade. It has developed and deployed new, mobile ICBMs and SLBMs and may be building a new heavy bomber. Beijing can no longer credibly make the case that its forces are so small—and intended only for a secure, retaliatory deterrent—that they need not be included in arms-control negotiations. China, as President Xi has made public, is determined to become a world power. Beijing is challenging the U.S. throughout the

Asia-Pacific, and nuclear weapons are a central component of its plans. China increasingly poses a challenge for U.S. extended deterrence in Asia. It is imperative that if U.S. nuclear forces are to be limited, Chinese forces must also be limited.

Arms-control disciples have long treated arms-control agreements as ends in themselves and, once negotiated, as sacrosanct, as with the now defunct ABM treaty. Perhaps for this reason, too often negotiations have produced unsatisfactory treaties that have channeled strategic arms competition in ways that have proven inimical to U.S. security interests. We can no longer base our positions on disarmament ideology or misplaced nostalgia for the familiar ways of the Cold War. Arms control can contribute to our national security, but only if it reduces the dangers of the current security setting. Arms control must look forward, not backward—unlike New START, which, although negotiated 20 years after the fall of the Berlin Wall, continued the traditional pattern of Cold War treaties.

Today's disciples will reject the desiderata described above as "nonnegotiable" while frantically calling for the immediate extension of New START, warning, like Chicken Little, that the sky will fall if we don't act immediately. But the contrary view is gaining increased support. The new realities are clearly recognized by a growing number of observers, including in the U.S. Congress. Senators Cotton and Cornyn and Representative Cheney last year introduced legislation that forbids the expenditure of any funds to extend New START unless both Chinese and Russian weapons are included in the extended agreement.

The U.S. needs a pragmatic approach that considers arms control as one of a wider set of tools that together support a broader strategy that encompasses developing the new nuclear and missile-defense capabilities prescribed by the recent DoD posture reviews. Only in this way can arms control serve our national security interests. That we must move beyond the tired nostrums of Cold War arms control to address today's dangerous nuclear environment should surprise no one.

Nuclear Deterrence and Low-Yield Nuclear Weapons

By Mark B. Schneider, Ph.D.

The Trump administration's 2018 Nuclear Posture Review assessed both U.S. nuclear capabilities and the threats that Russia, China, and other potential adversaries pose to the U.S. and allied security. Among its policy recommendations was the deployment of a small number of low-yield nuclear weapons on the Trident SLBM. The Trump administration's argument rested on increasing the credibility of our nuclear deterrent, and should deterrence fail, giving the president a broader range of credible options with which to respond to a nuclear or WMD attack on the U.S. homeland or on our allies. Opponents of President Trump's recommendations argue that low-yield nuclear weapons (a) increase the likelihood of nuclear war, (b) are unnecessary because high yield nuclear weapons and/or conventional weapons can deter low-yield nuclear attack, and (c) will ignite an arms race. Opposition to low-yield nuclear deterrence is often combined with recommendations to dramatically reduce the size of the U.S. nuclear deterrent.

To better understand the Trump administration's decision to deploy low-yield nuclear weapons, it is necessary to examine Russian and Chinese nuclear doctrine and the role that low-yield weapons play in it. The arguments set forth by minimum deterrence advocates will be addressed in greater detail below.

CONVENTIONAL VS. NUCLEAR WEAPONS

Maximizing the deterrence of nuclear and other forms of WMD attack must be the highest U.S. military priority; failure to do so could result in millions of deaths or even the destruction of the United States, its allies, and most of their populations. There is no substitute for nuclear weapons to deter nuclear and other forms of WMD attack because of the destructiveness of WMD. Arms control has eliminated the U.S. in-kind deterrent capability to chemical and biological attack but has retained adversary capabilities to launch such attacks.

It is increasingly suggested that precision conventional weapons can substitute for nuclear weapons. This is technical nonsense. The yield difference between existing conventional weapons and nuclear weapons pound for pound is as high as several million to one.[41] With even low-yield weapons it could be thousands to one. In 1999, Russian Colonel-General Vladimir Muravyev, then deputy commander of the Strategic Missile Forces, said, "They [nuclear weapons] are capable of nullifying the combat qualities of all modern conventional systems."[42] Russia's strategic nuclear weapons modernization since that time shows that the approach remains active.

Nuclear weapons have a great psychological impact. It is always possible for an aggressor to come up with some theory of victory for a conventional conflict, but it is much more difficult to do this in the context of nuclear warfare. While it is technically true that a wide variety of outcomes are possible in a nuclear conflict, this view is generally subject to ridicule. The inability of conventional weapons to attack effectively hard and deeply buried targets (HDBTs) associated with the foreign WMD threat is a critical limitation from the standpoint of assurance and damage limitation. Accuracy is always important, but it does not solve all military problems and GPS guidance is fragile.

The argument that a small, inflexible, high-yield nuclear force will substantially reduce the cost of nuclear deterrence is technically invalid. Expense is a poor excuse for keeping a small force. As then Deputy Secretary of Defense Ashton Carter pointed out in 2013, "nuclear weapons don't actually cost that much."[43] Even the pro-minimum-deterrence Federation of American Scientists admits that "with a stockpile of some 500 warheads, the size and cost of the weapons complex would only be a little smaller than what is proposed for a stockpile of 3,000 to 3,500 weapons."[44] As retired U.S. STRATCOM Commander Admiral Richard Mies has pointed out, nuclear weapons have very high destructive power for five percent of the defense budget.[45]

THE RUSSIAN VIEW OF WAR AND NUCLEAR WEAPONS

The idea of a major war with the West over natural resources appeared in the 2009 edition of Russia's National Security Strategy: "Under conditions of competition for resources, it is not excluded that arising problems may be resolved using military force, and that the current balance of power on the borders of Russia and its allies may be disturbed."[46] This belief is very dangerous because of the low Russian nuclear use threshold and its continuously advanced nuclear capabilities.

The year following issuance of Russia's National Security Strategy, then First Deputy Defense Minister Colonel-General Vladimir Popovkin stated that strategic nuclear forces, including early warning capability and aerospace defenses (missile defense, air defense, and ASAT) were

Russia's first priority and "precision weapons" were its second priority.[47] The Russians talk about "precision weapons" rather than "precision conventional weapons" because all of its precision missiles "are dual-capable or have nuclear analogs."[48] Russian military strategy is based on the view that the U.S. and NATO are the enemy and a major war with nuclear weapons use is possible. In January 2017, Defense Minister General Sergei Shoigu stated Russia will "continue a massive program of nuclear rearmament, deploying modern ICBMs on land and sea, [and] modernizing the strategic bomber force."[49] Weeks later, he said that strategic nuclear forces were Russia's "unconditional priority" because "nuclear weapons guarantee that Russia can deter any aggression of any foreign state."[50]

As far back as 1999, Colonel-General Muravyev stated that "the deterrent actions of strategic forces...[involve] strikes with both conventional and nuclear warheads with the goal of de-escalating the military conflict," and Russian forces "should be capable of conducting 'surgical' strikes...using both highly accurate, super-low yield nuclear weapons, as well as conventional ones."[51] Also, in 1999, Russian First Deputy Atomic Energy Minister Viktor Mikhailov said, "a 'new generation' of low-yield nuclear weapons 'can really be used in case of any large-scale military conflict.'"[52] In 2001, he supported the development of "low and super-low yield nuclear weapons and precision weapons with nuclear warheads."[53]

A now declassified CIA report from August 2000 stated, "Senior Russian military officers have advocated the use of highly accurate, super-low yield nuclear weapons in Russian military journals such as *Military Thought* and *Armeyskiy Shornik*."[54] It also said, "Recent statements on Russia's evolving nuclear weapons doctrine lower the threshold for first use of nuclear weapons and blur the boundary between nuclear and conventional warfare."[55] Another declassified CIA report observed, "A number of articles [in the Russian press] suggest that Russia is developing low-yield warheads with enhanced radiation that could be used on high-precision non-strategic weapons systems."[56] Russia is reportedly 20 years ahead of us in these weapons.

In 2002, noted Russian journalist Pavel Felgengauer wrote that in April 1999 the Russian Security Council approved a concept for developing and using "non-strategic low- and flexible-yield battlefield weapons," and that their yields would be tens or hundreds of tons of TNT.[57]

Since 2003, the official party line in Russia is that they do not have low-yield nuclear weapons. This is propaganda. Russia has reportedly developed and exercised the use of low-yield nuclear weapons. There were several Russian press reports concerning Russian nuclear weapons' first use in the Vostok 2010 military exercise. Indeed, the official newspaper of the Far East Military District said, "To suppress a large center of the separatists' resistance and to achieve minimal losses of the attacking troops a low-yield 'nuclear' attack was mounted against the enemy."[58] This report implies a threshold of nuclear weapons first use much lower than that contained in official Russian nuclear weapons use doctrine. Felgengauer, writing about the same exercise, reported that Russia used a nuclear-armed S-300 surface-to-air missile against a ground target.[59] This would very likely be a low-yield nuclear weapon since the primary mission of the missile is air defense, which requires a low-yield warhead.

Late in the Obama administration, the Defense Department pointed to the threat of Russian first use of low-yield nuclear weapons against the U.S. In 2016, Secretary of Defense Ashton Carter stated, "it's a sobering fact that the most likely use of nuclear weapons is not the massive nuclear exchange of the classic Cold War-type, but rather the unwise resort to smaller but still unprecedentedly terrible attacks, for example, by Russia or North Korea to try to coerce a conventionally superior opponent to back off or abandon an ally during a crisis."[60] In December 2016, a report by the Defense Science Board observed, "Russian doctrine is publicly stated as 'escalate to de-escalate' based on the assumption that its first use of low yield nuclear weapons against a conventionally superior NATO force would engender a halt to further aggression."[61]

The 2018 U.S. Nuclear Posture Review stated, "Russia's belief that limited nuclear first use, potentially including low-yield weapons, can provide such an advantage is based, in part, on Moscow's perception that its greater number and variety of nonstrategic nuclear systems provide a coercive advantage in crises and at lower levels of conflict. Recent Russian statements on this evolving nuclear weapons doctrine appear to lower the threshold for Moscow's first-use of nuclear weapons. Russia demonstrates its perception of the advantage these systems provide through numerous exercises and statements."[62]

RUSSIAN LOW-YIELD NUCLEAR CAPABILITY

In May 1999, Felgengauer wrote that Russia was developing "precision low-yield" nuclear weapons for strikes "anywhere in the world."[63] In March 2002, Felgengauer again reported that Russia was developing "superlow-yield weapons," penetrators, and "clean" nuclear weapons."[64] In December 2002, Viktor Mikhailov, then director of the Sarov nuclear weapons laboratory, stated that "the scientists are developing a nuclear 'scalpel' capable of 'surgically removing' and destroying very localized targets. The low-yield warhead will be surrounded with a super-hardened casing which makes it possible to penetrate 30–40 meters into rock and destroy a buried target—for example, a troop command and control point or a nuclear munitions storage facility."[65]

In 2008, actual Russian deployment of low-yield nuclear weapons (with yields between 50 and 200 tons of TNT) on strategic SLBMs was reported in the Russian press, including the state media (*Sputnik News* and *RIA Novosti*). These low-yield nuclear weapons included variable-yield and low-collateral-damage designs.[66]

In 2009, Vice Admiral Oleg Burtsev, then first deputy chief of the Russian Naval Staff, said that tactical nuclear weapons may be the wave of the future and "we can install low-yield warheads on existing cruise missiles."[67]

In December 2017, Dr. Philip Karber, president of the Potomac Foundation, stated that roughly half of Russia's 5,000 tactical nuclear weapons have been modernized with new sub-kiloton nuclear warheads for air defense, torpedoes, and cruise missiles.

In May 2019, DIA Ashley, director of the Defense Intelligence Agency, reported, "Russia's stockpile of non-strategic nuclear weapons—already large and diverse...is being modernized with an eye towards greater accuracy, longer ranges, and lower yields to suit their potential warfighting role."[68]

THE ROLE OF LOW-YIELD NUCLEAR WEAPONS IN CHINESE MILITARY STRATEGY

China is a communist dictatorship that practices extreme secrecy. Chinese secrecy about its nuclear capability opens the possibility of a major strategic surprise. The announced Chinese nuclear strategy of "no first use" is mainly propaganda. There is substantial evidence that China will use nuclear weapons first if it is in the Chinese Communist Party's perceived interest.

The 2018 Nuclear Posture Review report says that China, like Russia, has added "new types of nuclear capabilities to their arsenals, increased the salience of nuclear forces in their strategies and plans, and engaged in increasingly aggressive behavior, including in outer space and cyber space."[69]

CHINESE LOW-YIELD NUCLEAR WEAPONS

Estimates of the number of Chinese nuclear weapons range from a few hundred to thousands.[70] Most of the information we have about

Chinese nuclear capabilities comes directly or indirectly from Western and Asian governments. The Chinese government says little, although recently there has been a tendency to confirm the nuclear capability for the new missile systems. China has deployed a very large force of precision or near-precision guided ballistic missiles.[71] Chinese precision ballistic and cruise missiles clearly have the potential to deliver low-yield nuclear weapons effectively. For example, according to the 2018 Nuclear Posture Review report, China's new DF-26 IRBM is "a nuclear-capable precision guided...intermediate-range ballistic missile capable of attacking land and naval targets."[72] Any missile with sufficient accuracy to deliver a conventional warhead has more than enough accuracy to deliver an effective strike with low-yield nuclear weapons.

We know significantly less about Chinese nuclear capability than we know about Russia's because China is far more secretive. Even so, in the next 10 years, according to DIA Director Ashley, China "is likely to at least double the size of its nuclear stockpile."[73] Much of the dispute over the size of the Chinese nuclear arsenal involves the number of its nonstrategic nuclear weapons for its theater ballistic and cruise missiles. The House of Representatives' Cox Committee report stated in 1999 that China stole the design of the U.S. neutron bomb, an advanced low-yield/low-collateral-damage nuclear weapon also known as the enhanced radiation warhead, and tested a neutron bomb, which is almost always a low-yield weapon.[74]

Some of the highest estimates for the number of Chinese nuclear weapons come from Russia. Retired Colonel-General Viktor Yesin, the former commander of the Russian Strategic Missile Forces and currently a professor at Russia's Academy of Military Sciences, wrote that "there are probably 1600 to 1800 warheads in the Chinese threat missiles," which he lists as the DF-15, the DF-15A, the DF-11, the DF-11A, and the DH-10 cruise missile.[75] General Yesin also says that Chinese fighter aircraft can carry 5 to 20 kt nuclear weapons.[76] Under 5 kt is the definition of low-yield nuclear weapons contained in the legislation passed by the U.S. Congress in the 1990s that banned the American development of such weapons.[77] Another Russian report credits China's DF-15 with a neutron bomb warhead.[78] Reportedly, the Chinese neutron bomb test had a yield of 1 to 4 kt.[79] A Taiwanese defense publication reported that the Chinese DF-15 has a low-yield nuclear weapon for the purpose of an EMP attack.[80]

In the year 2000, Chinese Major General Wu Jianguo, a former associate professor and dean of the Chinese Antichemical Warfare Academy, reportedly gave "several proposals for new kinds of Chinese nuclear weapons, including a ground-penetrating nuclear weapon with an equivalent of 10 tons of TNT, an antimissile nuclear weapon with an equivalent of 100 tons of TNT, and a ground-to-ground and air-to-ground nuclear weapon with an equivalent of 1,000 tons of TNT."[81]

A declassified 1995 *National Intelligence Daily* report indicated that "China could be seeking to confirm the reliability of a nuclear artillery shell designed in advance of a nuclear test ban" in order to defend against Russian invasion or an amphibious landing.[82] Nuclear artillery tends to be relatively low-yield to minimize collateral damage.

THE NEED FOR A LOW-YIELD NUCLEAR DETERRENT

Minimum deterrence supporters are attacking the modest 2018 Nuclear Posture Review program to enhance our deterrent against Russian, Chinese, and potentially even North Korean or Iranian first use of relatively low-yield nuclear weapons. One of them characterized the low-yield Trident as "The World's Most Dangerous Nuclear Weapon," completely ignoring the reported Russian deployment of much lower yield strategic nuclear weapons as early as 2008 and Russian violations of the Presidential Nuclear Initiatives, begun by President George H. W. Bush in 1991, which were supposed to largely eliminate tactical nuclear weapons. Minimum deterrence advocates have reinvented some of the most foolish of the 1980s arguments that attempted to derail the Reagan administration's nuclear modernization programs. Had they been successful, there could have been a major war or even a nuclear war in the 1980s. Today, the threat is in some respects even greater than the Soviets in the 1980s because of the Putin factor (nuclear irresponsibility) and we now face a multipolar threat environment. The risk of war is increasing because of the Russian and Chinese nuclear buildup and our lack of a comparable response.

It is likely that Russia and China could engage in the first use of nuclear weapons if they believe it to be in their national interests. It is the job of the U.S. nuclear deterrent to ensure they do not reach this conclusion. Their potential nuclear first use will initially be very likely to involve low-yield weapons, particularly if the vocal U.S. minimum deterrence establishment manages to prevent the creation of an effective low-yield nuclear deterrent to low-yield nuclear attack. An inadequate deterrent exists today because of the lack of a clearly survivable low-yield nuclear capability. A low-yield deterrent based completely upon *non-alert* bombers and nuclear-capable fighter aircraft is inadequate because they are much too vulnerable to relatively small numbers of low-yield and/or low-collateral-damage nuclear strikes. Even if the bombers and fighters were put on alert, their undefended bases are potentially vulnerable to the Russian hypersonic nuclear missiles that are now becoming operational.

We need a sea-based low-yield deterrent for the same reasons we need a strategic nuclear triad with SLBMs. Considering the well-known U.S. aversion to collateral damage, which we broadcast every day in our military operations, the threat of a high-yield nuclear response to a low-yield nuclear attack lacks credibility. That type of deterrence threat is irresponsible because of the increased risk it would entail for no reason other than ideology. It stands in stark contrast to the last 60 years of U.S. defense policy that has been aimed at reducing the risk of escalation into an all-out or even large-scale nuclear exchange. It is ideologically driven, made worse by the budget-hawk reasoning that low-yield nuclear warheads are low cost (about $50 million for the low-yield Trident program). Indeed, the marginal cost is probably close to zero when compared to the money saved by not producing the same number of high-yield warheads. It is clear that we need both low- and high-yield nuclear weapons on every leg of our strategic triad and in our nonstrategic nuclear capability.

Low-yield nuclear weapons, particularly sub-kiloton weapons, but even a five or ten kiloton weapon, ensure that even with a ground-burst, lethal fallout will be limited to areas close to the point of detonation. Low-yield weapons vastly reduce the collateral damage from blast and heat. With standard types of high-yield nuclear weapons, there is no guarantee of limiting fallout to a small area and, hence, avoiding the possibility of large numbers of collateral casualties. With high-yield nuclear weapons, increasing the height of burst sufficiently so that the fireball does not come into contact with the earth will generally result in no lethal fallout. The key word here is *generally*. If the radioactive cloud generated by the nuclear detonation comes into contact with a rainstorm, the fallout effect, which is called "rainout," could be widespread and very lethal. Even at 5 kt the amount of fallout from rainout might be 1% to 5% of a high-yield nuclear bomb. If we deployed sub-kiloton warheads, the fallout would be less than 1%, and if we went to a low-collateral-damage design (minimum yield from fission), it could be virtually nothing. Adoption of a non-optimum high-altitude burst for high-yield nuclear weapons will reduce collateral damage from blast and heat somewhat, but the destruction could still be considerable. Moreover, doing this can reduce the military effectiveness of the device compared to a ground or subsurface burst with a low-yield nuclear weapon against some types of targets.

The argument has been made that the launch of a low-yield Trident would subject the Trident submarine to attack. This argument is largely bogus. The launch point of the missile would not likely be located with high accuracy and the submarine would not be in the same place when enemy missiles arrive. Moreover, U.S. missile defenses could be used to defend the submarine if necessary.

This alleged concern about the survivability of U.S. missile submarines would be touching except for the fact that minimum deterrence advocates often propose reducing the size of the U.S. missile submarine force to an extent that would do far more damage to our deterrent than any likely Russian missile strike. Moreover, minimum deterrence advocates are now departing from their standard argument that missile submarines are invulnerable, which they use to rationalize their argument for a reduced number of submarines.

According to Ambassador Steven Pifer, "The Russians could not tell whether a launched SLBM carried a W76-2 or a W76-1 (100 kilotons) or, for that matter, a W88 (450 kilotons) until the weapon (or weapons) detonated."[83] His apparent assumption is that the Russians would launch a high-yield nuclear strike while the Trident missile is still in flight. He also states, erroneously, that Russia could not tell where the missile or missiles were going. This is simply not true considering the capabilities of Russian early warning radars, which are good enough to support Russian missile defense. He completely ignores the implication of what he is proposing. If the only U.S. option, as he desires, is a high-yield ballistic missile response to a Russian low-yield nuclear missile strike, the Russians would be certain that the U.S. Trident missile launch would be conducting a high-yield attack. Moreover, in the scenario he postulated ("a few 'small' nuclear weapons" used against the Baltic states), a low-yield Trident response would be completely unnecessary. Bomber and dual-capable fighter aircraft could be used. The deterrent value of the low-yield Trident warheads would come into play in preventing the Russians from having the option of launching a larger, but still limited, low-yield attack against U.S. bomber bases and U.S. and NATO bases in order to destroy the American ability to retaliate against a low-yield nuclear attack in-kind.[84]

The "arms race" argument by arms control enthusiasts is also ridiculous when one considers that Russia reportedly started deploying low-yield strategic nuclear missile warheads a decade ago. We are playing catchup from a position of being well behind. Moreover, we are doing nothing about low-collateral-damage nuclear weapons. If Felgengauer is correct in his report that Russian missile warheads are variable-yield, we could be greatly outnumbered even with the Trump administration's low-yield program. The situation would be much worse if Dr. Phillip Karber is correct that the Russians now have 2,500 low-yield tactical or nonstrategic nuclear weapons.

Most of the Trump administration's proposals in the 2020 National Defense Authorization Act to improve the U.S. nuclear arsenal in the were approved by Congress in December 2019. See Chapter 10 for details.

Congressional cuts will lock in Vladimir Putin's nuclear advantage. As Rep. Mike Turner, ranking member of the House Armed Services Committee Subcommittee (HASC) on Strategic Forces stated, the HASC cuts to the nuclear weapons program would put us at "a significant disadvantage with regard to Russia by prohibiting funds for the deployment of a low-yield ballistic missile warhead."[85] This is particularly true when the low-yield warhead elimination is seen in the context of the HASC's cuts to other nuclear programs, which could ultimately result in about a 100-to-1 Russian advantage in nuclear weapons numbers.

CONCLUSION

The minimum deterrence attacks on the Trump administration's decision to deploy a small number of relatively low-yield nuclear weapons are striking in their shrillness against a broadly bipartisan defense policy. The Trump administration's 2018 Nuclear Posture Review decisions have been endorsed by the senior leadership of the Defense Department and endorsed by the National Defense Strategy Commission. If Bill Gertz is correct in his report that the yield of the low-yield Trident warhead (W-76 Mod 2) is 5 to 10 kt (6.5 kt according to the Union of Concerned Scientists), the weapon is not even technically a low-yield nuclear weapon under the less-than-5-kt definition. Since the arguments against low-yield nuclear warheads are disingenuous, it may be that the hidden agenda is to prevent any U.S. nuclear response to a Russian nuclear attack on the U.S. and its allies. In light of the proclivities of President Vladimir Putin—to say nothing of Russia's still poorly understood propaganda and disinformation strategy to influence American policies and decision-making—the impact of this could well be further Russian nuclear escalation. The minimum deterrence agenda of "no first use" of nuclear weapons is openly to prevent any nuclear response to a chemical or biological attack, no matter how destructive the attack. Hence, the hidden agenda of opposition to the low-yield nuclear Trident deterrent program could very well be the same regarding any nuclear weapons attack.

Why EMP Weapons Represent a Growing and Existential Threat to the United States

By Peter Vincent Pry, Ph.D.

Given that the United States faces a host of emerging threats from nuclear, biological, chemical, radiological, and enhanced conventional WMDs, why should the U.S. be more concerned, or as concerned, about nuclear EMP attacks than these other threats?[86] There are numerous reasons why—and why EMP is an attractive attack option for America's adversaries.

It is first important to understand what EMP is and the grave damage it could inflict on the United States.

WHAT IS EMP?

For the purposes of national security, EMP is a phenomenon in which a burst of highly charged radio waves—electromagnetic radiation—disrupts or destroys electrical and electronic systems without physical destruction of people, infrastructure, and environment. EMP can come from natural sources like the sun and lightning, but natural EMP can usually be blocked or channeled and rendered harmless.

As a national defense threat, EMP is a product of a nuclear weapons blast, against which our defenses are few. EMP attacks can be relatively small and localized through low-altitude or surface-level bursts of nuclear energy, or large enough to cover the entire United States when done from a high altitude. An enemy can inflict EMP damage across extensive territory by firing a missile to detonate one or more nuclear weapons at a very high altitude over the target. The electromagnetic radiation released from the detonation, not blast and heat, "fries" electric power and transmission systems and all electronics that are not specifically hardened against attack, as well as thousands of low-orbit satellites that support American defense, communications, and commerce.

The United States and Soviet Union independently discovered the EMP phenomenon more than six decades ago when they began testing nuclear weapons and their effects on military equipment and civilian infrastructure. Localized "source region" EMP (SREMP) was observed during the first U.S. ground-burst nuclear test. Electronic infrastructure inside the source region (typically within 2–5 km of the blast) was harmed by the initial radiation output (gamma, x-rays, neutrons), producing electron currents and air conductivity—sources for the SREMP.

Surface-burst nuclear tests in the 1950s and 1960s demonstrated that SREMP can disrupt and upset electronic systems over 100 miles away and in deeply buried structures. SREMP can even propagate currents into and through power lines or telecommunication lines in areas well outside of the source region and into every device connected to them. This means that EMP generated by even a surface burst nuclear weapon could cause widespread, long-term regional loss of power and communications.

This is old science. Both the United States and the Soviet Union understood that a high-altitude nuclear detonation could produce similar electromagnetic effects as surface bursts. In the 1960s, both nations conducted high altitude EMP (HEMP) tests and found that the resulting infrastructure damage was far worse than originally predicted. These tests revealed that the EMP generated by a nuclear weapon detonated at 30 km or higher produces a super-energetic radio wave that has three components, designated by the U.S. scientific-technical community as E1, E2, and E3.

E1 is caused by gamma rays emitted by a nuclear warhead that knock electrons off molecules in the upper atmosphere, causing the electrons to rotate rapidly around the lines of the Earth's magnetic field, a phenomenon termed the Compton Effect. The E1 component of nuclear EMP is a shockwave, transmitting thousands of volts of energy in mere nanoseconds of time. E1 EMP has a short, high-frequency wavelength that can couple directly into small conductors, like transformers, automobiles, and personal computers. E1 is unique to nuclear weapons and is too fast and too energetic to be arrested by protective devices used for lightning.[87]

The E2 component of a nuclear EMP is comparable to lightning in its energetic content and medium (milliseconds) frequency and wavelength. Protective devices used for lightning are effective against E2.

E3 is caused by the fireball of a nuclear explosion or from a solar flare. The expanding and then collapsing fireball cause the Earth's magnetic field to oscillate. This oscillation generates electric currents in the very large conductors that can couple into the low frequency, long (seconds) wavelength part of the EMP that is E3. The E3 waveform can couple directly into conductors with at least one dimension of great length. Electric power and telecommunications lines that run for kilometers in many directions are ideally suited for receiving E3. Although E3 appears to deliver little energy compared to E1, just volts per meter, this is multiplied manifold by power and telecommunications lines that are typically many kilometers long. This multiplication of energy builds up E3 currents that can melt extremely high voltage (EHV) transformers, typically designed to handle 750,000 volts. Small electronics can also be destroyed by E3 if they are connected in any way to an E3 receiver—like a personal computer plugged into an electric outlet.

Any nuclear weapon detonated at high altitude (30 km or higher) will generate a powerful electromagnetic pulse propagating at the speed of light from the point of detonation to the Earth's visible horizon, covering a vast region (about 600 km or 370 mi in radius at a burst height of 30 km) with an energy field that can black out electric grids and damage unprotected electronics. Higher-yield nuclear weapons can generate more powerful and more damaging EMPs, but all EMP fields are dangerous. Nuclear weapons specialized for EMP can be very low yield in terms of blast but generate the most powerful and most dangerous fields.

The Congressional EMP Commission has assessed that Russia, China, and North Korea have such "Super-EMP" weapons.[88]

WHAT COULD EMP DO TO THE U.S.?

An EMP attack would probably cause more material and costly damage and affect more Americans than any other attack option executable with one or a few missiles.[89] If damage to U.S. civilian infrastructure is sufficiently widespread, it may not be recoverable. Under these circumstances, compared to other attack options, an EMP attack could conceivably kill most Americans in the long run—possibly up to 90% of the population—through the disruption of communications, logistics, and economic activity.[90]

An EMP would shut down everything necessary for modern life: cars, trucks, trains, ships, aircraft; electric power, cell phones and data centers, and all other electronic communication; hospitals; banks and all electronic means of payment, investment, and commerce; governance and law enforcement; and the production and distribution of food, fuel, and medicine.

In cities and the most densely populated regions of the country, a single EMP attack could result in murderous social strife among people struggling to pillage and stockpile food, fuel, and other necessities to survive. That social breakdown would follow with tens or hundreds of millions of people suffering slow and agonizing deaths from mass starvation, exposure, and the diseases and pestilence that accompany famine and the decay of the unburied dead.

ADVANTAGES THAT EMP OFFERS U.S. ADVERSARIES

A capability of EMP attack offers numerous technical, operational, strategic, and political advantages over other nuclear and WMD options. The main advantage is that it allows rogue states to leverage their smaller and less sophisticated nuclear and missile programs to inflict catastrophic damage on their enemies.

EMP attack can compensate for the difficulties of mastering complex technical issues associated with missile reentry vehicle design, fusing, accuracy, range, intelligence regarding target location, collateral damage, and missile defense penetration.

Strategically and politically, a capability of EMP attack is among the most credible WMD threats of deterrence or blackmail because it would attack electronics, not physical infrastructure and people.

In contrast to the limited effect radius of other WMD options, EMP can neutralize entire regional or national infrastructures that are vital to U.S. military strength and societal survival. It could also challenge the integrity of allied coalitions.

An EMP attack could pose a retaliatory dilemma for the United States since EMP is an asymmetric threat and more dangerous to the electronically advanced West than to underdeveloped Third World rogue states or Russia and China, whose critical infrastructures are better protected.

EMP is also a force multiplier that, if used in conjunction with other WMD options, would greatly increase their effectiveness.

EMP ATTACK: TECHNICAL AND OPERATIONAL ADVANTAGES

Intercontinental ballistic missiles armed with EMP warheads do not require the sophistication that they would need if armed with other types of weapons. This makes EMP-armed ICBMs cheaper and easier to develop for rogue regimes or other actors.

An EMP attack does not face the challenge of atmospheric reentry, as do other ballistic missile attack options. In order to hit targets on the other side of the planet, ballistic missiles are fired into space on steep trajectories. During atmospheric reentry, missile warheads are exposed to intense heat, reaching hundreds of degrees Fahrenheit, and to G-forces that would stress the weapons package and internal mechanisms of the warhead. These are daunting engineering challenges for states like Iran and North Korea, which have little or no opportunity to flight-test reentry vehicles.

A nuclear weapon delivered for EMP would be detonated at least 30 km above the Earth's surface, potentially hundreds of kilometers into the atmosphere, depending upon the desired coverage, field strengths, and other targeting requirements for an EMP attack, eliminating the need for atmospheric reentry. This sharply reduces the engineering challenges for an EMP attack.

By contrast, other attack options require warhead penetration of the atmosphere, in most cases to within less than 1 km from Earth's surface. An attack relying on nuclear blast, biological, chemical, or enhanced conventional weapons—such as fuel-air explosive bombs or submunition bomblets—requires virtually complete atmospheric penetration. Rogue state warheads, expected to be delivered inaccurately by missiles with primitive guidance systems, could be rendered even more inaccurate by winds and uneven heat shield ablation. Lightning, storms, hail, and other meteorological conditions could also damage or destroy poorly designed warheads.

An EMP attack does not require detonation at a precise altitude or ground detonation. Fusing mechanisms for an EMP burst could tolerate inaccuracies of many kilometers without degrading EMP attack effectiveness. This would also benefit states with smaller and less sophisticated missile and nuclear programs.

By contrast, missile attack options requiring atmospheric reentry require robust and accurate fusing mechanisms for detonation at a desired altitude.

EMP attack does not require precise intelligence about target location and would better cope with moving targets than other missile attack options. An EMP's effective radius can be hundreds or even thousands of kilometers. Uncertainty about precise target coordinates and moving targets such as aircraft, ships, and ground forces would not be a significant impediment to a successful EMP attack.[91]

By contrast, because the effective radius of nuclear blast, biological, chemical, and enhanced conventional attack is several kilometers or less, precise intelligence about target location is required for successful attack by these means. Rogue states may lack adequate geodetic and other data to support sufficiently accurate delivery of a weapon against even fixed targets, let alone mobile targets. Reliable real-time intelligence is required to attack mobile targets. An aircraft carrier, for example, could move more than 40 mi off missile aimpoint based on relatively fresh intelligence only one hour old.

Rogue state missiles are expected to have primitive guidance systems, making them inherently inaccurate.[92] Additional inaccuracies because of inadequate intelligence about target location would further decrease the effectiveness of missile attack options relying on nuclear blast, biological, chemical, or enhanced conventional weapons.

By contrast, an ICBM attack employing nuclear blast or biological, chemical, or enhanced conventional weapons against U.S. military targets, given a missile's circular error probable (CEP) of 15–30 km, would most likely prove ineffective. (CEP is a measure of a missile's accuracy.)

A high-value military target in the United States that a rogue state might consider worth attacking with an ICBM is Whiteman AFB, with runways supporting B-2 operations that cover an area of about 10 km^2. This is one of the largest, easiest to hit, most high-value military targets in the United States. Postulate that a North Korean ICBM with CEP 5–30 km could deliver a 20 kt nuclear warhead, a biological warhead containing anthrax, a chemical warhead containing sarin nerve gas, or an enhanced conventional warhead with anti-runway submunitions. The odds any of these would be delivered close enough to Whiteman AFB to place a lethal radius on runways is less than 3%.[93]

Even if used as nonmilitary terror weapons for attacking cities at intercontinental ranges, nuclear blast, biological, and chemical warheads would be of problematical lethality if delivered by an ICBM with very poor accuracy, as would be expected for rogue state missiles.

An EMP attack would enable missiles to attack targets that ordinarily, using any other attack option, are beyond their range. The higher an EMP burst occurs, the further and wider the "horizon" of effect. For example, a nuclear weapon burst at 100 km high will project an EMP field on the Earth's surface to a radius of roughly 1,000 km or 600 mi. A nuclear burst 300 km high would project an EMP field radius approximately 2,500 km or 1,500 mi, meaning that a single EMP burst at that altitude over the central United States would have a devastating effect coast-to-coast.

Because of the great radius of EMP effects, missiles used for this attack option could threaten targets far beyond their normal operational range. For example, a North Korean No Dong medium-range ballistic missile (MRBM) with an estimated range of 1,300 km could, in effect, extend its range to 2,300 km, 3,800 km, or more in an EMP attack. Iran's Shahab III MRBM, which cannot quite reach Europe with its 1,300-km range, could reach far into Europe if used in an EMP attack.

Thus, EMP attack offers potential adversaries a means to, in effect, convert short-range ballistic missiles into medium-range missiles, convert MRBMs into IRBMs, and convert IRBMs into ICBMs.

An EMP attack would likely pose less collateral risk to the aggressor in a theater of operations compared to other missile attack options. Because the attacker knows precisely when it will execute an EMP attack, it can target the attack and prepare its own forces in ways that minimize damage to its own troops and operations. Except for damage to electrical systems and dependent infrastructure, EMP attack leaves no persistent aftereffects. The same cannot be said of nuclear blast, biological, and chemical weapons.

In the event North Korea used WMDs against U.S. and South Korean forces near the demilitarized zone, the North could seriously impede its own military invasion of the South. Nuclear blast would likely block roads and destroy bridges and railways. "Hot zones" of radiation and biological and chemical contaminants could also impede North Korean offensive operations. Radioactive, biological, and chemical contamination can last years, reducing the value of conquered territory. Wind and weather could possibly return contamination to the aggressor's homeland. EMP attack poses fewer or none of these problems.

Similarly, suppose China uses nuclear weapons to open a corridor for air and naval strikes on an American aircraft carrier by blasting U.S. ships and allied defending an aircraft carrier group. Chinese strike forces would have to operate through the nuclear targeted area in order to attack. Nuclear strikes on Aegis cruisers and other picket ships would pose a significant risk of collateral damage to Chinese strike forces and would likely impede operations by obscuring targets visually and electronically. In contrast, an EMP attack could be timed and located to spare Chinese forces from collateral damage and would create no atmospheric perturbations that could interfere with targeting and strike operations.

An EMP attack would be less vulnerable to and more effective against missile defenses than other missile attack options. Since an EMP attack does not require atmospheric reentry and can be executed in a way that allows a standoff distance from the target of potentially thousands of kilometers, such an attack would be able to lessen the effectiveness of missile defenses or perhaps elude them altogether. An EMP also poses a significant threat to missile defenses that are highly dependent upon radars, satellites, and other sophisticated electronic systems. The United States abandoned its Safeguard anti-ballistic missile (ABM) system in the 1970s in part because of concerns that the system would be unable to cope with EMP effects.

By contrast, missile attack options relying on nuclear blast, biological, chemical, or enhanced conventional weapons will have to run the full gamut of U.S. theater or national missile defenses that might exist. An advanced adversary might well provide its nuclear weapons with a salvage fusing option for EMP attack, just in case the warhead is intercepted above the atmosphere.

STRATEGIC AND POLITICAL ADVANTAGES OF AN EMP ATTACK

EMP promises a "bigger bang for the buck" by simultaneously threatening all military electronic systems in a broad region, potentially across an entire theater of operations, with one weapon. A single nuclear blast, biological, chemical, or enhanced conventional missile attack would destroy only a single target. An EMP weapon offers much more strategic value than other WMDs. An adversary would probably prefer to use an EMP weapon to degrade, disrupt, or neutralize all U.S. military forces on the battlefield and beyond rather than use a WMD weapon to destroy a single airfield but leave overall U.S. war fighting capabilities generally intact.

EMP threatens the most valuable U.S. military targets: satellites; command, control, and communications; and high-tech weaponry dependent upon sophisticated electronics. Official unclassified U.S. military doctrine acknowledges that sensors and information systems are now more important to U.S. military strength than weapons and delivery systems.[94] Destroying a U.S. military base and killing U.S. troops with a nuclear blast, biological or chemical agents, or enhanced conventional weapons might be likened to a body blow in a boxing contest—a blow that can be returned manifold and much harder by the United States as long as its electronic central nervous system remains intact. An EMP attack, by contrast, constitutes a blow against the U.S. military's central nervous system.

An EMP also promises "bigger bang for the buck" in attacking U.S. society. A nuclear blast, biological, or chemical attack might damage or destroy a U.S. city and promptly kill hundreds or thousands of Americans. However, except in the case of a massive attack by Russia or China on U.S. cities, the damage to the United States economy would probably be recoverable and loss of life comparatively limited. An EMP is probably the most damaging use of a single or small number of missiles. An EMP attack threatens the civilian electronic infrastructures—power, telecommunications, transportation, computers, and information systems—that are the foundation of the United States economy, political system, and social order. An EMP attack would probably cause more material and costly damage and affect more Americans than any other attack option executable with one or a few missiles.[95] If damage to U.S. civilian infrastructure is sufficiently widespread, it may not be recoverable. Under these circumstances, compared to other attack options, an EMP attack could conceivably kill more Americans in the long run—possibly up to 90% of the population, through starvation, disease, and social strife that would result from the destruction of the electronic networks of agriculture, logistics, medicine, finance, commerce, and governance.[96]

The threat or fact of an EMP attack upon U.S. forces or society would confront the United States with a retaliatory dilemma.[97] Perhaps worse, the asymmetrical risk inherent in an EMP threat may confer on U.S. adversaries a credible deterrent, as during the Cold War, but a deterrent that keeps the United States—not adversaries—contained. U.S. military commitments to allies and willingness to act militarily has, up to now, been in an environment where rogue and non-state actors could not pose a lopsided, vital threat to the U.S. homeland or to U.S. forces overseas. The credible capability to threaten the United States asymmetrically through EMP attack could change the whole calculus of risk and benefit for the United States that is the foundation of its current defense and foreign policy as the world's only superpower.

Because an EMP attack would target electronics, not lives, and probably cause relatively little immediate loss of life (compared to a nuclear or biological attack on a city), the United States may be hard-pressed to justify retaliating with weapons of mass destruction. An adversary might credibly argue to the international community that an EMP attack, delivered amid a grave crisis or war, is a desperate act of "political signaling"—a warning shot intended to prevent or de-escalate conflict and return parties to negotiation, lest WMD escalation ensues that causes "real" damage and loss of life.

The first use of atomic or nuclear weapons since Nagasaki is sure to be a potent political symbol, greatly elevating the visibility and international significance of any crisis or conflict. If an adversary uses a missile to blast or contaminate a U.S. city, it will instantly become a pariah and be abandoned by the international community to its fate. But if an adversary launches an EMP attack that "spares" American lives, especially if accompanied by a "peace offensive," an international community anxious to avoid escalation might be recruited politically to the adversary's side.

Thus, EMP attack offers adversaries some prospect to use nuclear missiles for maximum counterforce or countervalue effectiveness, while wrongly being credited by the international community as displaying restraint, and possibly escaping American nuclear retaliation. An EMP attack may be the nuclear war equivalent of "having your cake and eating it, too."[98]

An EMP threat or actual attack, as part of a sound divide-and-conquer strategy, can be credible against all or most of the members of an allied coalition because of EMP's broad area coverage. North Korea, for example, could use a single missile to make an EMP attack that would affect U.S. military forces in the theater, South Korea, and Japan—the allied principals in a regional crisis or conflict. The cooperation of Seoul and Tokyo are indispensable to U.S. military operations on the Korean peninsula. Allied collective and individual political resolve, not just the political will of the United States, would be tested by an EMP attack. A coalition is only as strong as its weakest link.

An EMP attack would probably increase the effectiveness of all other WMD attack options. For example, an attack employing biological or chemical weapons against one or several U.S. cities will be limited by the effectiveness of federal, state, and local agencies and emergency services in detecting and responding to that threat. EMP, by contrast, would disrupt power and communications, paralyzing U.S. capabilities to respond to a WMD biological or chemical attack, so that greater damage and more casualties would be produced with less physical destruction. As the United States achieves greater preparedness against biological, chemical, and other WMD threats, an EMP attack that disrupts U.S. emergency preparations would be an increasingly valuable yet economical force multiplier for all WMD attack options.

Finally, no single or several dozen targets could be destroyed by nuclear blast, biological, chemical, or enhanced conventional weapons that could decisively cripple the United States military or society. **Only an EMP attack can threaten the indispensable vitals of the United States society or military so comprehensively and offer some promise, however slim, of victory.**

EMP SCENARIOS[99]

Many of the potential advantages of EMP attack are widely known to the general public. EMP scenarios have even been represented, with varying degrees of realism, in popular works of fiction and on television. Defense and academic threat analyses have created scenarios for EMP attack spanning a broader range of military-political conditions than probably any other employment option for nuclear weapons. This implies something about the potential wide utility of EMP attack compared to other nuclear attack options and may also imply something about the relative likelihood of an EMP attack.

An unclassified study by the U.S. Defense Threat Reduction Agency (DTRA), *NBC Scenarios: 2002–2010*, postulates a scenario for EMP attack.[100]

An unclassified DTRA study posits several other scenarios of EMP attacks where EMP is either the primary lethal effect or a secondary "bonus" effect. DTRA's High-Altitude Nuclear Detonations (HAND) Against Low Earth Orbit Satellites *("HALEOS")* report warns that a nuclear detonation above the atmosphere could destroy satellites in low Earth orbit (LEO) that are commercially and militarily critical to the United States: "One low-yield (10–20 kt), high-altitude (125–300 km) nuclear explosion could disable—in weeks to months—*all* LEO satellites not specifically hardened to withstand radiation generated by that explosion."[101]

The DTRA *HALEOS* report suggests numerous generic scenarios for a high-altitude nuclear attack, including "regional nuclear war," a "nuclear warning shot in a regional conflict," an "effort to damage adversary forces/infrastructure with electromagnetic pulse," or as an attempt to save the warhead from missile defenses by "salvage fusing" when intercepted. According to DTRA, a high-altitude nuclear attack could also be a "deliberate effort to cause economic damage with lower likelihood of nuclear retaliation." Such an attack might be executed by a "rogue state facing economic strangulation or imminent military defeat" or in order to "pose an economic threat to the industrial world without causing human casualties or visible damage to the economic system," according to the study.[102]

Academic literature is also replete with plausible scenarios for EMP attack. For example, Sean J. A. Edwards argued long ago that EMP attack is the best nuclear option for Third World states that must confront the technologically superior U.S. Army of the 21st century. Whereas most EMP scenarios are aimed at U.S. air, naval, or space assets, the EMP attack that Edwards postulated is aimed at making the high-tech U.S. Army vulnerable to Third World conventional forces:

> There are two main reasons why a nascent nuclear power would be willing to use one of its precious nuclear weapons for a HEMP attack. First, it is the best asymmetric strategic choice in a regional crisis where an adversary's conventional forces are arrayed against U.S. forces. The HEMP-conventional attack offers a chance for a quick victory while avoiding any serious risk of U.S. nuclear retaliation. Second, the U.S. Army will become increasingly more vulnerable to HEMP.... a costly battle that inflicts casualties on U.S.

forces might raise the costs of intervention above a level considered acceptable for Americans. The trick is to achieve a "Tet Offensive" or "Mogadishu" reaction, not a "Pearl Harbor" reaction.[103]

Edwards contended a Third World state could combine an EMP attack with an attack by its conventional forces to achieve victory without provoking U.S. nuclear retaliation:

A symmetric strategy like a conventional attack has no hope for success against a Force XXI Army with information dominance. Asymmetric strategies which directly use weapons of mass destruction (WMD), such as dropping a fission bomb directly on U.S. troops, would backfire and anger the American public, and probably provoke a devastating U.S. nuclear response.... An adversary's best option is to avoid using nuclear weapons directly on U.S. troops and instead employ them as a sort of massive electronic warfare tool to beat the United States at its own game. By integrating a HEMP attack on U.S... [command, control, communications, and intelligence] assets with a conventional attack on the projected U.S. forces in the region, a U.S. adversary would stand a good chance of inflicting heavy casualties on a deaf and blind American force, ill prepared to fight without its information and communication advantages.104

The Heritage Foundation's Jack Spencer assesses in his paper *America's Vulnerability to A Different Nuclear Threat: An Electromagnetic Pulse*[105] that, like Edwards argued,

The motivation for a rogue state to use its limited nuclear arsenal in an EMP strike against the United States is simple: It maximizes the impact of its few warheads while minimizing the risk of retaliation.... Because EMP attacks are less risky...such attacks are far more likely to occur in this era of nuclear proliferation than they were at any time during the Cold War.[106]

Eleven generic scenarios provide a framework for thinking about circumstances that might lead to an EMP attack:

- **An EMP attack against U.S. strategic C3 and nuclear forces to debilitate U.S. nuclear retaliatory capabilities.** This was the chief scenario for EMP attack during the Cold War and is still relevant today. An EMP precursor to massive counterforce attack could prevent or slow execution of U.S. ICBMs and bombers so that they could be destroyed before launching. An EMP could impede operation of U.S. SSBNs and other naval forces at sea by degrading their CONUS-based C3.[107]

- **An EMP attack against U.S. general purpose forces in CONUS.** North Korea, Iran, Iraq or another adversary engaged in a theater of conventional war with the United States might calculate that an EMP attack against U.S. conventional forces in CONUS would be the most effective option, militarily and strategically. U.S. plans for theater war assume the U.S. will be able to reinforce forward deployed ground, air, and naval forces from other theaters and especially from the United States. An EMP attack early in a crisis or conflict could paralyze those military forces or logistical assets—like airlift capabilities—intended to reinforce the theater from the United States.

- **An EMP attack against U.S. and allied general purpose forces in theater.** An EMP attack could support a general offensive against U.S. and allied forces on the battlefield. In South Korea, the Middle East, and Taiwan, U.S. and friendly forces present are vastly outnumbered by potential adversaries. For example, on the Korean peninsula, North Korea's million-man army with 5,000 tanks is opposed by 37,000 U.S. troops. An adversary might calculate that an EMP attack against U.S. and allied forces in theater would enable him to more successfully exploit his local numerical preponderance and achieve a quick victory. Adversaries might also calculate that an EMP attack is the only way of achieving a battlefield victory, or stalemate, against the high-tech U.S. military *after* reinforcements have arrived in theater. U.S. aircraft carriers, viewed by potential adversaries as the backbone of U.S. power projection capabilities, would be high on the list of targets for in-theater EMP attacks.

- **An EMP attack against U.S. civilian infrastructure.** EMP attack effectiveness is most problematic against strategic forces and C3 (that have received the most hardening), less problematic against general purpose forces (that have received some hardening), and least problematic against civilian infrastructure (that has received the least hardening). An EMP attack against U.S. civilian infrastructure is sure to be catastrophic.[108] The objective of such an attack might be to make the economic and domestic political price of war too high for the United States. An EMP attack might be calculated to permanently alter U.S. foreign policy by turning the American people against the nation's traditional global military presence and toward an isolationist "fortress America" mentality.

Vengeance should not be underestimated as a possible motive for EMP attack on U.S. civilians. Elites in North Korea and Iran are not likely to survive losing a war to the United States and may want to inflict the greatest possible injury.

- **An EMP attack against allied civilian infrastructure.** In a war in which the United States military effort depends upon a coalition of allies, an adversary might try to divide the coalition by launching an EMP attack against the civilian infrastructure of one or more U.S. allies. The objective would be to turn one or more allies against the war by making the cost of continuing the conflict, in the view of those allies, not worth the effort. In most imaginable major wars that could occur overseas, the United States would require allied political and military support. An adversary may believe, with some justification, that it is easier to break the will of U.S. allies than to test the will of the United States itself.

- **An EMP attack for salvage fusing.** An adversary concerned that its missiles might be intercepted by defenses might fuse nuclear warheads to detonate upon interception. Since interception of a ballistic missile is most likely to occur at high altitude, the detonating warhead would produce an EMP attack that might still reach the intended target or other targets of value. Salvage fusing for an EMP attack might also be employed as a backup option should the missile fail for mechanical reasons during flight at high altitude. Such failures have been a common feature during flight-tests of primitive missiles deployed and under development by such states as North Korea and Iran.

- **An EMP attack "warning shot."** An EMP attack could be performed during a crisis or conflict to exploit U.S. and international fear of nuclear weapons in order to achieve a favorable outcome. The democratic international community perceives a vital interest in preserving longstanding non-use of nuclear weapons in war. Confronted with an EMP "warning shot," many U.S. allies, and many U.S. citizens, might prefer that the United States yield in a crisis or war rather than risk further nuclear escalation.

- **An EMP attack miscalculation.** A potential adversary may mistakenly believe, based on false intelligence, that the United States is about to strike with nuclear or advanced conventional weapons, and launch an EMP attack to preempt the impending "U.S. aggression." EMP attack would be a particularly attractive option if the adversary had some uncertainty about its intelligence indicating an imminent U.S. threat. An EMP would disrupt U.S. forces and warn Washington against aggression—if aggression is contemplated—but inflict the least number of casualties on U.S. forces if the intelligence proves false.

- **An EMP attack as a "bonus" to an anti-satellite operation.** An adversary might calculate that the most militarily effective option would be to degrade or destroy U.S. low-orbiting satellites with a high-altitude nuclear detonation. Most satellites are low-orbiting. Under this "bonus" scenario, an EMP attack would be secondary to the attack against the satellites. A high-altitude nuclear detonation against the satellites would also generate an EMP that could degrade U.S. and allied forces or civilian infrastructure.[109]

- **An EMP attack between other parties.** An EMP attack during war between other nations, not involving the United States, could nonetheless threaten U.S. assets, forces, or allies. For example, nuclear war could arise between India and Pakistan, China and India, Russia and China, Israel and Iran, or other combinations. The detonation of a nuclear weapon in space for an EMP could damage or destroy U.S. satellites, eliminating trillions of dollars' worth of investment and commerce, even if the United States is not the intended target.

- **An inadvertent EMP Event.** Catastrophic failure of a rogue-state nuclear missile, not necessarily aimed at the United States or U.S. forces, could nonetheless trigger a nuclear detonation at high altitude, generating an EMP event injurious to the United States, U.S. forces or allies, and American investment and trade.

FOREWARNED

Some may argue state or non-state actors would not dare violate longstanding international norms against employing nuclear weapons—even for an EMP attack—under any conceivable scenario.

It is well to remember that the United States, arguably the world's most humanitarian nation, is also the only nation ever to use nuclear weapons. Today, most Americans still agree that the U.S. government's decision to drop atomic bombs on Hiroshima and Nagasaki in 1945 was, under the circumstances, militarily and morally right.

The political norms of North Korea, Iran, China, and Russia are no guarantee against any nuclear scenario conceivable, including EMP attack.

The Trump Nuclear Posture Review

By Fred Fleitz

This monograph discusses serious problems facing America's nuclear deterrent and proposed steps by the Trump administration to address them in the 2018 Nuclear Posture Review (NPR). This chapter discusses the 2018 NPR considering the analysis presented in previous chapters and prospects for the NPR's proposals to be implemented and succeed.

In February 2018, the Trump administration issued an assessment of America's nuclear weapons arsenal in the NPR. The Nuclear Posture Review was chartered in October 1993 to determine the role of nuclear weapons in U.S. security strategy and the status of America's nuclear arsenal. There has been an NPR during every U.S. presidency since the Clinton administration. The Obama Nuclear Posture Review was issued in 2010.

The Trump administration's NPR had to address two major problems concerning U.S. nuclear weapons.

The first problem was undoing the naïve approach of the Obama administration's NPR, which mostly ignored the state of America's nuclear arsenal and instead promoted President Obama's "Road to Zero" policy: a pledge that the U.S. would not use nuclear weapons against non-nuclear weapon states, calls for reducing U.S. nuclear arms and not developing new weapons; and other recommendations that reflected the Left's hostility to the very existence of America's nuclear arsenal.

The second problem is much more serious and concerns the failure of multiple presidents to arrest the deterioration of the U.S. nuclear arsenal and update America's nuclear policies in response to new security threats to the United States, including significantly different threats from the nuclear arsenals of U.S. adversaries.

The Obama NPR could have been worse except that it needed to be cleared by then Secretary of Defense Robert Gates, who had a far more clear-eyed view of American national security than most of his Obama administration colleagues. As a result, this document was largely aspirational and only delayed action to improve and update the U.S. nuclear deterrent. There were also provisions to maintain the U.S. nuclear arsenal and a plan to invest over $80 billion on it between 2010 and 2020.

THE OBAMA NPR: A SMALL BUT DAMAGING STEP BACKWARD

In some ways the 2010 NPR resembled those issued by other administrations. It called for preventing nuclear proliferation and nuclear terrorism; maintaining strategic deterrence; strengthening regional deterrence; and sustaining a safe, secure, and effective nuclear arsenal. The Obama NPR purported to provide a long-term strategy to be conducted by multiple administrations and Congresses to address a "changed and changing international security environment."

The 2010 NPR said the threat of global nuclear war had become remote but also that the risk of nuclear attacks had surged due to an increased risk from nuclear terrorism. The Review cited a growing risk of nuclear proliferation that could enable terrorist groups like al Qaeda to steal nuclear materials or buy them on the black market.

Obama's NPR was seen by many as a significant shift from prior NPRs since it renounced the development of new nuclear weapons. This overruled the initial position of Secretary of Defense Gates by freezing U.S. nuclear weapons development, resulting in worsened readiness problems for the U.S. nuclear arsenal that had been growing for decades.

The Obama NPR also ended the policy of ambiguity about when the United States would use nuclear weapons by pledging that the U.S. would not use such weapons against states in compliance with the Nuclear Nonproliferation Treaty (NPT) even if they attacked the United States with biological, chemical, or cyber weapons. At the same time, Obama officials offered a confusing qualification to this policy by saying the Review included "the option of reconsidering the use of nuclear retaliation against a biological attack, if the development of such weapons reached a level that made the United States vulnerable to a devastating strike," according to the *New York Times*.[110] President Obama also rejected demands by many on the Left that he declare the U.S. would never be the first state to use nuclear weapons.

Obama officials said there were new options to retaliate against cyber, chemical, or biological weapons attacks using high-power conventional weapons. President Obama said such threats could be deterred with "a series of old and new conventional weapons."[111]

At the core of President Obama's NPR was his commitment to a nuclear weapons-free world and his belief that the United States must lead by example to achieve this. That is, if the United States moved away from relying on nuclear weapons for defense, other nations would follow suit and begin to eliminate their nuclear arsenals.

This was one of President Obama's many naïve approaches to national security. Jamie Fly, President of Radio Free Europe/Radio Liberty, said this about Mr. Obama's approach in a 2010 National Review symposium article: "This is pure fantasy. Iran and North Korea do not care how many nuclear weapons the United States possesses, and a promise to use nuclear weapons against them only if they are in noncompliance with the international nonproliferation regime will not cause them to modify their behavior."[112]

In the same article, Brian Kennedy, chairman of the Committee on the Present Danger: China and president of the American Strategy Group, took issue with the Obama NPR's "bold and bizarre assertion that Russia is not our enemy" and noted that "the Russians continue to build ever more advanced ballistic nuclear missiles, supply Iran with the technology and know-how to develop such weapons for use against the United States and Israel, and, with the Communist Chinese, seek to marginalize the United States and its allies."

Moreover, the Obama NPR's intention to reduce the U.S. nuclear arsenal and its nuclear umbrella that protects about 30 countries worked against President Obama's nuclear nonproliferation goals by encouraging these states to develop their own nuclear arsenals.

Like prior NPRs, the Obama NPR recommended maintaining nuclear warheads through LEPs and certifying the U.S. nuclear arsenal through the Stockpile Stewardship Program (SSP). Despite criticism of the SSP's limitations and a growing number of reports that Russia and China were engaged in low-level nuclear tests in violation of the CTBT to develop new nuclear weapons, the Obama administration utterly rejected the idea of resuming nuclear tests to maintain and develop the U.S. nuclear arsenal and instead celebrated the 20th anniversary of the SSP in 2015 "as one of the nation's greatest achievements in science and security" and claimed that "today, nuclear explosive testing has been replaced by an annual assessment process that examines each weapons system in scientific and engineering detail in a manner that is instilled with scientific rigor and allows peer review."[113]

President Obama was accused of reneging on his nuclear disarmament pledge in 2013 when he agreed to an $11 billion modernization plan to convert 200 B61 gravity bombs stored in Belgium into guided weapons that could be delivered by stealth F-35 fighters as well as the F-1 and F-15. Arms control activists faulted the president for developing new weapons by this move, a charge that Obama officials disputed. Other critics accused the Obama administration of spending billions of dollars on nuclear modernization to buy off members of Congress.[114]

The 2013 move to modernize the B61 nuclear weapon reflected the half-hearted nature of President Obama's nuclear disarmament strategy. Mr. Obama believed in his Road to Zero policy but was not prepared to fight for it or pay any significant political price to advance this strategy. Like many of the president's other national security policies, his nuclear strategy was mostly aspirational.

Even though President Obama's nuclear strategy was not fully implemented, deterioration of the U.S. nuclear arsenal and America's nuclear advantages may have accelerated during the Obama years due to neglect of this crucial program.

THE TRUMP NPR: FIVE MAJOR CHALLENGES FACING THE U.S. NUCLEAR DETERRENT

President Trump's 2018 NPR rejected the approach of the Obama NPR by making a case that although America's long-term goal is a world without nuclear weapons, because there is no prospect of this happening in the foreseeable future and due to growing threats from the nuclear arsenals of other states, America must be prepared for nuclear weapons to play an enduring role in U.S. national security. The 2018 NPR noted in the introduction that "global threat conditions have worsened markedly since the most recent 2010 NPR, including increasingly explicit nuclear threats from potential adversaries. The United States now faces a more diverse and advanced nuclear-threat environment than ever before, with considerable dynamism in potential adversaries' development and deployment programs for nuclear weapons and delivery systems."

Mark Schneider noted earlier in this monograph that according to the 2018 Nuclear Posture Review, China's new DF-26 intermediate-range ballistic missile is "a nuclear-capable precision guided...intermediate-range ballistic missile capable of attacking land and naval targets." Schneider also wrote that Russia's belief that limited nuclear first use, potentially including low-yield weapons, can provide an advantage is based, in part, on Moscow's perception that its greater number and variety of nonstrategic nuclear systems provide a coercive advantage in crises and at lower levels of conflict.

The NPR also noted other increasingly aggressive behavior by U.S. adversaries, including in outer space and cyber warfare, as well as nuclear programs by North Korea and Iran.

The Trump NPR expressed the administration's concerns about an evolving and uncertain international security environment, noting that while the United States has continued to reduce its reliance on nuclear weapons, other states, including Russia and China, have moved in the opposite direction. According to the NPR, there has been a rapid deterioration in the threat environment since the 2010 NPR. It also asserted that "previous U.S. nuclear policies were established amid a more benign nuclear environment and more amiable Great Power relations."

President Trump's NPR explicitly rejected the benign view of Russia of the Obama NPR. Critics of the Review, such as Adam Mount with the Federation of American Scientists, rejected this and other aspects of the Trump NPR as reflecting a "dark and threatening world" and claimed its call to expand U.S. reliance on nuclear weapons endangers international security.[115]

Conditions for when the United States could use nuclear weapons was a major change in the Trump NPR by stating that the United States could use them in response to "significant non-nuclear attacks," including "attacks on U.S., allied or partner population or infrastructure." Other cases in which the U.S. could employ nuclear weapons include "attacks on U.S. or allied nuclear forces, their command and control, or warning and attack assessment capabilities."

To respond to a world of growing nuclear threats, the 2018 NPR also called for developing a diverse, flexible, and modern U.S. nuclear arsenal, including the following:

- Reforms and improvements to U.S. nuclear enterprise personnel.
- Development of low-yield nuclear weapons to match Russian nuclear strategies, including modifying some submarine-launched ballistic missiles with low-yield warheads.
- Development of a modern nuclear-armed sea-launched cruise missile to give the U.S. additional flexibility and diversity in defense options and to offer an incentive to Russia to negotiate a reduction in its nonstrategic nuclear weapons.
- Modernization of nuclear command, control, and communications.
- Significant new spending to overcome the effects of the effects of old age and underfunding of the U.S. nuclear infrastructure.

OUTLOOK FOR THE TRUMP NPR

Although the House Democratic majority attempted to significantly reduce funding to implement the Trump NPR and deny funding for low-yield nuclear weapons in the 2020 National Defense Authorization Act, Senate Democrats sided with their Republican counterparts in approving most of the Trump administration's funding requests related to the NPR, and the final bill, which passed on December 17, 2019 reflected the Senate version. President Trump signed the NDAA into law the next day. The Trump administration's budgets request for the U.S. nuclear program in the 2021 NDAA proposed even high spending to improve America's nuclear deterrent.

The 2020 NDAA approved nearly the entirety of the Trump administration's proposed budget request for programs to sustain and rebuild nuclear-armed missiles, submarines, and bombers and their supporting infrastructure, including $2.2 billion to build a fleet of 12 new ballistic missile submarines, $3 billion to build a fleet of at least 100 new long-range bombers, $558 million to build a new ICBM system, and $713 million to replace the existing air-launched cruise missile. $253 million was allocated to resume processing plutonium and producing plutonium pits. A further $12.5 billion was approved for nuclear weapons activities conducted by the NNSA, an increase of $49 million above the budget request and $1.4 billion more than last year's appropriation.

The 2020 NDAA also included language by congressional Democrats requiring additional reports to Congress and justifications for certain nuclear activities, such as independent studies on the benefits and risks of a U.S. no-first-use policy, the risks of nuclear terrorism and nuclear war, and the plan to replace the W78 ICBM warhead with the W87-1. The NDAA also requires reports on the risks of executing the W87-1 program, the estimated cost and impact of building a new sea-launched cruise missile warhead, and the current status and future of the B83-1 gravity bomb.

The Trump administration's 2021 NDAA budget request, released on February 11, 2020, proposed an additional $46 billion in nuclear weapons spending, a 19% increase. This includes an additional $28.9 billion for NNSA and a $17.7 billion increase for nuclear research, development, testing and evaluation projects, including:

- $4.4 billion for Columbia-class submarines
- $4.2 billion for nuclear command, control and communications
- $2.8 billion for the B-21 bomber
- $1.5 billion for the Ground Based Strategic Deterrent

- $1.2 billion for the Trident II missile life extension program
- $500 million for the long-range standoff cruise missile
- $110 million for nuclear-related costs on the F-35 Joint Strike Fighter
- $50 million on the B61-12 nuclear bomb tail kit

The 2021 NDAA also proposes funds for the five major warhead modernization programs: the B61-12 Life Extension Program, the W80-4 Life Extension Program, the W88 Alteration 370, the W87-1 Modification Program and the W93, a new submarine-launched nuclear warhead. How the 2021 NDAA request will fare in Congress was unclear when this publication went to print.

Meanwhile, the Trump administration is looking at initiatives beyond the 2018 NPR. It withdrew from the INF Treaty in 2019. Some Trump advisers do not want the administration to renew the New START treaty when it expires in 2021. There have also been reports that the Trump administration may be considering preparing to resume underground nuclear testing and "unsigning" the 1996 CTBT.

Former Obama NSC official Stephen Andreasen asserted this in a June 2019 *Washington Post* op-ed when he wrote that "Quietly and under a shadow of unease at home and abroad, the Trump administration is opening the door to U.S. resumption of underground nuclear explosive testing in response to Russian cheating."[116] Such a move would be hugely controversial and probably would not be attempted by the Trump administration before the 2020 presidential election.

The Trump NPR could salvage and maintain America's nuclear arsenal. But its dire situation could also worsen significantly depending on U.S. political developments. It is still too soon to predict the success of the 2018 NPR and how much it will improve America's nuclear deterrent. This review will need 8 to 10 years to be fully implemented, which means it is unlikely to have a significant effect on the U.S. nuclear program if Mr. Trump loses the 2020 election. America's nuclear arsenal will likely suffer a major setback with a Trump election loss if—as seems likely—his Democratic successor reverts to a nuclear strategy like the Obama NPR.

It is crucial that we modernize our nuclear weapons and pursue a sound nuclear weapons policy regardless of who is elected the next president because as we saw during the Obama administration, the real world has a way of teaching responsibility no matter the campaign promises.

About the Authors

FRED FLEITZ is the president and CEO of the Center for Security Policy. He served in 2018 as a deputy assistant to President Donald Trump and chief of staff to National Security Adviser John Bolton. Before his White House position, Fleitz was senior vice president of the Center for Security Policy. He previously served in U.S. national security positions for 25 years with the CIA, the DIA, the Department of State, and House Intelligence Committee staff.

DR. MICHAELA DODGE is a research scholar at the National Institute for Public Policy. Prior to joining the National Institute, Dr. Dodge worked at the Heritage Foundation as a research fellow for Missile Defense and Nuclear Deterrence from 2010–2019. She left Heritage to serve as Senator Jon Kyl's senior defense policy advisor. Additionally, she was a Publius Fellow at the Claremont Institute in 2011 and participated in the Center for Strategic and International Studies PONI Nuclear Scholars Initiative Program. Dr. Dodge received a Ph.D. from George Mason University in 2019. She earned her Master of Science in Defense and Strategic Studies degree from Missouri State University in 2011.At Missouri State, Dr. Dodge was awarded the Ulrike Schumacher Memorial Scholarship for two years. She received a bachelor's degree in international relations and defense and strategic studies from Masaryk University, Czech Republic.

AMBASSADOR ERIC S. EDELMAN retired as a career minister from the U.S. Foreign Service. He is currently a Roger Hertog Practitioner in Residence at Johns Hopkins SAIS and Counselor at the Center for Strategic and Budgetary Assessments.

FRANK GAFFNEY is the founder and executive chairman of the Center for Security Policy, a former official in the Reagan Defense Department and host of Secure Freedom Radio. Under Gaffney's leadership, the Center became nationally and internationally recognized as a reputable resource for foreign and defense policy matters. Mr. Gaffney was the deputy assistant secretary of defense for Nuclear Forces and Arms Control Policy from 1983 to 1987. Following that he was nominated by President Reagan to become the assistant secretary of defense for International Security Policy. He is also currently the director of Save the Persecuted Christians.

DR. JOHN C. HOPKINS began his career as a student at Los Alamos National Laboratory. He received both his bachelor's and doctoral degrees from the University of Washington and returned to the Laboratory in 1960. He participated in 5 atmospheric nuclear tests in the Pacific and later some 170 tests at the Nevada Test Site. In 1974, Hopkins was appointed as the Nuclear Test Division leader and he was later appointed as the Laboratory's associate director for the Nuclear Weapons Program. Throughout his career, he was involved in nuclear policy and nuclear history and has authored books and papers in these fields. He served as an advisor to the Department of Energy and the State and Defense departments and has worked with the nuclear weapons programs of Britain, France, China, and Russia.

PETER HUESSY is a defense analyst specializing in congressional, budget, and policy developments on nuclear deterrent policy, strategic nuclear modernization, terrorism, counterterrorism, immigration, state-sponsored terrorism, missile defense—especially U.S.-Israel joint defense efforts, arms control, proliferation, and space power. He is also president of his own defense consulting firm, GeoStrategic Analysis, founded in 1981, and was the senior defense consultant at the National Defense University Foundation for 22 years.

AMBASSADOR ROBERT JOSEPH is a well-known arms control expert who served in senior U.S. government national security posts, including ambassador to the U.S.-Russian Commission on Nuclear Testing, under secretary of state for arms control and international security, National Security Council senior director for nonproliferation, principal deputy assistant secretary of defense for international security policy, deputy assistant secretary of defense for nuclear forces and arms control policy, and nuclear policy/planning officer at U.S. Mission to NATO. He is currently a senior scholar at the National Institute for Public Policy.

DR. MATTHEW KROENIG is the deputy director of the Scowcroft Center for Strategy and Security at the Atlantic Council and a tenured associate professor of government and foreign service at Georgetown University. In 2019, he was named one of the top 25 most-cited American political scientists of his generation. He is the author or editor of seven books, including *The Logic of American Nuclear Strategy* (Oxford University Press, 2018). He previously worked in several positions in the U.S. Department of Defense and the intelligence community and as a fellow at the Council on Foreign Relations, Harvard University, and Stanford University. He is a life member of the Council on Foreign Relations and holds an M.A. and Ph.D. in political science from the University of California at Berkeley.

Dr. Mark B. Schneider is a senior analyst with the National Institute for Public Policy. Before his retirement from the Department of Defense Senior Executive Service, Dr. Schneider served in a number of senior positions within the Office of Secretary of Defense for Policy, including principal director for forces policy; principal director for strategic defense, space, and verification policy; director for strategic arms control policy; and representative of the secretary of defense to the Nuclear Arms Control Implementation Commissions. He also served in the senior Foreign Service as a member of the State Department Policy Planning Staff. Dr. Schneider earned his Ph.D. in history at the University of Southern California and his Juris Doctorate from George Washington University. He was admitted to the bar of Washington, DC, in 1977 and of Maryland in 1978. He specializes in missile defense policy, nuclear weapons, deterrence, strategic forces, arms control, and arms control verification and compliance issues.

Dr. Peter Vincent Pry is executive director of the EMP Task Force on National and Homeland Security, a congressional advisory board dedicated to achieving protection of the United States from electromagnetic pulse, cyberattack, mass destruction terrorism, and other threats to civilian critical infrastructures on an accelerated basis. Dr. Pry is also director of the United States Nuclear Strategy Forum, an advisory board to Congress on policies to counter weapons of mass destruction.

Endnotes

1 Kristensen, M., & Korda, M. (2019). Russian nuclear forces, 2019. *Bulletin of the Atomic Scientists*, *75*(2), pp. 73–84.
https://doi.org/10.1080/00963402.2019.1580891

2 U.S. Department of Defense. (2018, February). *Nuclear posture review 2018.*
https://dod.defense.gov/News/SpecialReports/2018NuclearPostureReview.aspx

3 Ibid.

4 Lendon, B. (2013, March 19). *U.S. flies B-52s over South Korea.* CNN.
https://www.cnn.com/2013/03/19/world/asia/korea-b-52s/index.html
(accessed June 7, 2019).

5 Weisgerber, M. (2017, September 13). *At US nuclear weapons base, Mattis signals support for triad.* Defense One.
https://www.defenseone.com/business/2017/09/us-nuclear-weapons-base-mattis-signals-support-triad/140987/

6 National Nuclear Security Administration. (2016, March). *Prevent, counter, and respond—A strategic plan to reduce global nuclear threats, FY 2017–FY 2021: Report to Congress.* U.S. Department of Energy.
https://www.energy.gov/sites/prod/files/2017/09/f36/NPCR%2520FINAL%25203-29-16%2520%28with%2520signatures%29_Revised%25204%252020_Redacted%5B1%5D.pdf

7 National Nuclear Security Administration. (2019, February). *Infrastructure modernization.* U.S. Department of Energy.
https://www.energy.gov/sites/prod/files/2019/02/f59/2019-02-14-FACTSHEET-Infrastructure-Modernization.pdf

8 One of the B-2 bombers crashed in 2008, leaving the United States with 20 aircraft.

9 Hennigan, W. J. (2013, August 19). Upgrades aim to extend B-52 bombers' already long lives. *Los Angeles Times.* https://www.latimes.com/business/la-xpm-2013-aug-19-la-fi-ageless-b52-bomber-20130819-story.html

10 Osborn, K. (2019, May 29). B-21 stealth bomber: The air force's ultimate "black" program (armed with nukes). *The National Interest.*
https://nationalinterest.org/blog/buzz/b-21-stealth-bomber-air-forces-ultimate-black-program-armed-nukes-59982

11 Harvey, J. R. (2019, May 24). *U.S. nuclear command and control for the 21st century.* Nautilus Institute NAPSNet Special Report.
https://nautilus.org/napsnet/napsnet-special-reports/u-s-nuclear-command-and-control-for-the-21st-century/

12 For more detail on the arguments presented in this essay, see Kroenig, M. (2018). *The logic of American nuclear strategy: Why strategic superiority matters.* Oxford University Press.

13 Smith, A. (writer), & Brown, B. (director). (2017, February 26). Trump calls for nuclear dominance [TV series episode]. In C. Jones, D. Williams, & E. Johnson (Executive Producers), *Weekends with Alex Witt*, MSNBC. http://www.msnbc.com/weekends-with-alex-witt/watch/trump-calls-for-nuclear-dominance-885291075918

14 John Mueller as cited in Kroenig, M. (2018). *The logic of American nuclear strategy*, Oxford University Press, p. 17.

15 Erlanger, S. (2019, August 8). Are we headed for another expensive nuclear arms race? Could be. *New York Times*. https://www.nytimes.com/2019/08/08/world/europe/arms-race-russia-china.html

16 Kroenig, M. (2016) US nuclear weapons and nonproliferation: Is there a link? *Journal of Peace Research, 53*(2), pp. 166–179.

17 Ashton Carter, as cited in Kroenig, M. (2018). *The Logic of American Nuclear Strategy*, p. 181.

18 Glanz, J. (2000, November 28). Testing the aging stockpile in a test ban era. *New York Times*.

19 Kristensen, H. M. (2019). French nuclear forces, 2019. *Bulletin of the Atomic Scientists, 75*(1), pp. 51–55.

20 Kristensen, H. M., & Korda, M. (2018). Indian nuclear forces, 2018. *Bulletin of the Atomic Scientists, 74*(6).

21 Kristensen, H. M., Norris, R. S., & Diamond, J. (2018). Pakistani nuclear forces, 2018. *Bulletin of the Atomic Scientists, 74*(5). https://doi.org/10.1080/00963402.2018.1507796

22 Jehl, D. (1993, March 13). U.S. seeking UN pressure to compel North Korea to honor treaty. *New York Times*.

23 Ibid.

24 White House. (2019, February 1). President Donald J. Trump to withdraw the United States from the Intermediate-Range Nuclear Forces (INF) Treaty [Fact sheet].

25 Dodge, M. (2019, May 21). *New START and the future of U.S. national security*. The Heritage Foundation. https://www.heritage.org/arms-control/report/new-start-and-the-future-us-national-security

26 Ibid.

27 Isachenkov, V. (2019, February 20). Vladimir Putin warns new Russian weapons will target U.S. *Washington Times*.

28 U.S. Department of Defense. (2019, July 21). Remarks by Under Secretary of Defense for Policy John Rood at the Aspen Security Forum.

29 Dodge, M. (2019, May 21). New START and the future of U.S. national security. The Heritage Foundation. https://www.heritage.org/arms-control/report/new-start-and-the-future-us-national-security

30 Payne, K. B. (2011, January 18). Postscript on New START. *National Review*. https://www.nationalreview.com/2011/01/postscript-new-start-keith-b-payne/

31 Dodge, M. (2019, May 21). New START and the future of U.S. national security. The Heritage Foundation. https://www.heritage.org/arms-control/report/new-start-and-the-future-us-national-security

32 Trachtenberg, D. (2019, March 28). House Arms Services Committee Subcommittee on Strategic Forces Hearing: Fiscal Year 2020 Priorities for Department of Defense Nuclear Activities.

33 Estimates of pit life vary and have also been estimated to be as long as 150 years. For a discussion of this issue, see Medalia, J. E. (2014, February 21) *U.S. nuclear weapon "pit" production options for Congress*. Congressional Research Service. https://fas.org/sgp/crs/nuke/R43406.pdf

34 Fisher, R. D. (2019, May 14). Breakfast seminar remarks. Mitchell Institute.

35 This material is from extensive conversations with Mark Schneider of NIPP over the past few months as well as similar conversations and email exchanges with James Howe; both put together extensive material about current and projected Russian nuclear weapons as well as sharing with me numerous formal presentations and unpublished material under their own names.

36 Ibid.

37 Ashley, R. P. (2019, May 29). *Russian and Chinese nuclear modernization trends: Remarks at the Hudson Institute* [Transcript of speech]. https://www.dia.mil/News/Speeches-and-Testimonies/Article-View/Article/1859890/russian-and-chinese-nuclear-modernization-trends/

38 Gertz, B. (2019, August 1). Stratcom: China rapidly building up nuclear forces. *Washington Free Beacon*. https://freebeacon.com/national-security/stratcom-china-rapidly-building-up-nuclear-forces/

39 Ibid.

40 Zhao, T. (2019, March). China in a world with no U.S.-Russia treaty-based arms control. In V. Manzo, *Nuclear arms control without a treaty: Risks without New START*, Center for Naval Analyses, Strategy, Policy, Plans, and Programs Division, pp. 118–125.

41 Mies, R. (2012, Spring) Strategic deterrence in the 21st century, *Undersea Warfare*, *48*, p. 16. https://igs.berkeley.edu/sites/default/files/files/events/mies831strat.in_21st_century_0.pdf

42 Quoted in Schneider, M. B. (2006). *The nuclear forces and doctrine of the Russian Federation*. National Institute Press. p. 22. http://www.nipp.org/Publication/Downloads/ Publication%20Archive%20PDF/Russian%20nuclear%20doctrine%20--%20NSF%20for%20print.pdf

43 U.S. Department of Defense. (2013, July 18). *Remarks by Deputy Secretary of Defense Carter at the Aspen Security Forum*. http://www.defense.gov/transcripts/transcript.aspx?transcriptid=5277

44 Federation of American Scientists. (2010, July 13). DOE plan promises additional nuclear reductions, but few cost savings [Fact sheet]. http://www.fas.org/press/_docs/fact_sheet.html

45 Mies, R. (2012, Spring). Strategic deterrence in the 21st century. *Undersea Warfare, 48*, p. 17.

46 Russian Federation. (2009, May 12). Russia's national security strategy to 2020 (translated by rustrans.wikidot.com). paragraph 12. Last edited September 17, 2012. http://rustrans.wikidot.com/russia-s-national-security-strategy-to-2020

47 Interview with Vladimir Popovkin. *Rossiyskaya Gazeta.* http://russiadefence.englishboard.net/t1294-interview-with-vladimir-popovkin, (2010, July 12).

48 Johnson, D. (2018, February). *Russia's conventional precision strike capabilities, regional crises, and nuclear thresholds.* Lawrence Livermore National Laboratory. p. 57. https://cgsr.llnl.gov/

49 Felgengauer, P. (2017, January 19). Kremlin learning to navigate Washington's new unpredictability. *Eurasia Daily Monitor, 14*(3). https://jamestown.org/program/kremlin-learning-navigate-washingtons-new-unpredictability/

50 "Development of strategic nuclear forces is unconditional priority – Shoigu." (2017, February 21). *Interfax.*

51 Quoted in Howe, J. R. (2016, February 17). Exploring the dichotomy between New START treaty obligations and Russian actions and rhetoric. Vision Centric, Inc. https://www.exchangemonitor.com//wp-content/uploads/2016/04/Thu-9am-Future-Nuclear-Arms-Control-Stacked.pdf

52 Quoted in Schneider, M. (2008). The future of the U.S. nuclear deterrent. *Comparative Strategy, 27*(4), p. 348. http://www.tandfonline.com/doi/abs/10.1080/01495930802358539.

53 Quoted in Schneider, M. (2008). The future of the U.S. nuclear deterrent. *Comparative Strategy, 27*(4), p. 347.

54 Office of Transnational Issues. (2000, August 30). *Evidence of Russian development of new sub-kiloton nuclear warheads.* Central Intelligence Agency.

55 Ibid.

56 Office of Russian and European Analysis. (2000, June 22). Russia: [Deleted]. Central Intelligence Agency. http://www2.gwu.edu/~nsarchiv/NSAEBB/NSAEBB200/20000622.pdf

57 Felgengauer, P. (2002, March 14). Bomber makers trade union. *Moscow Times.* http://www. themoscowtimes.com/opinion/article/bomb-makers-trade-union/247805html

58 Parker, J. W. (2011, January). *Russia's revival: Ambitions, limitations, and opportunities for the United States.* Institute for National Strategic Studies. p. 23. http://www.dtic.mil/dtic/tr/fulltext/u2/a546683.pdf

59 Felgengauer, P. (2010, July 16). Russia seeks to impose new ABM treaty on the US by developing BMD. *Eurasia Daily Monitor, 7*(136).

https://jamestown.org/program/russia-seeks-to-impose-new-abm-treaty-on-the-us-by-developing-bmd/

60 U. S. Department of Defense. (2016, September 26). *Remarks by Secretary Carter to troops at Minot Air Force Base, North Dakota* [transcript of speech]. http://www.defense.gov/News/Transcripts/Transcript-View/Article/957408/remarks-by-secretary-carter-to-troops-at-kirtland-afb-new-mexico

61 Defense Science Board. (2016, December). *Seven defense priorities for the new administration.* p. 23. https://www.acq.osd.mil/dsb/reports/2010s/SevenDefense_Priorities.pdf.

62 U.S. Department of Defense. (2018, February). *Nuclear posture review 2018.* pp. xi–xii. https://media.defense.gov/2018/Feb/02/2001872886/-1/-1/1/2018-NUCLEAR-POSTUREREVIEW-FINAL-REPORT.PDF.

63 Quoted in Schneider, M. B. (2006). *The nuclear forces and doctrine of the Russian Federation.* National Institute Press. p. 15. http://www.nipp.org/Publication/Downloads/ Publication%20

64 Ibid.

65 Quoted in Schneider, M. (2008). The future of the U.S. nuclear deterrent. *Comparative Strategy, 27*(4), p. 348.

66 For more detail and documentation, see Schneider, M. B. (2018, March 12). Deterring Russian first use of low-yield nuclear weapons. *Comparative Strategy.* https://www.realcleardefense.com/articles/2018/03/12/deterringrussianfirstuseoflowyieldnuclearweapons113180.html.

67 Russian Federation will increase role of tactical nuclear weapons on multirole nuclear submarines. *Gazeta.* (2009, March 23).

68 Ashley, R. P. (2019, May 29). *Russian and Chinese nuclear modernization trends: Remarks at the Hudson Institute* [Transcript of speech]. https://www.dia.mil/News/Speeches-and-Testimonies/Article-View/Article/1859890/russian-and-chinese-nuclear-modernization-trends/

69 U.S. Department of Defense. (2018, February). *Nuclear posture review 2018.* p. 1. https://dod.defense.gov/News/SpecialReports/2018NuclearPostureReview.aspx

70 Ministry of National Defense, Taiwan. (2011). *Section 2 PRC military capabilities and threats.* Taiwan: Republic of China. http://2011mndreport.mnd.gov.tw/en/info04. html; Yesin, V. (2012). *On China's nuclear potential without underestimation or exaggeration.* Asian Arms Control Project. http://www.scribd.com/doc/98667133/ YESIN-China-s-Nuclear-Potential; Arbatov, A. (2012, July 8). Russia: Problems in involving PRC in nuclear arms limitation, transparency talks. *Voyenno-Promyshlennyy Kuryer Online* (translated by World News Connection); China may have 1,600-1,800 nuclear munitions – experts. (2012, September 28). *Interfax-AVN Online* (translated by World News Connection). A similar conclusion was reached by U.S. expert Dr. Phillip Karber. See Wan, W. (2011, November 29). Georgetown students shed light on China's tunnel system for nuclear weapons. *Washington Post.*

http://articles. Washington post.com/2011-11-29/world/35280981_1_nuclear-weapons-georgetown-students-military journals

[71] National Air and Space Intelligence Center. (2013). *Ballistic and cruise missile threat.* NASIC Public Affairs Office. p. 10. http://www.afisr.af.mil/shared/media/document/AFD-130710-054.pdf.

[72] Ibid., p. 11.

[73] Ashley, R. P. (2019, May 29). *Russian and Chinese nuclear modernization trends: Remarks at the Hudson Institute* [Transcript of speech]. https://www.dia.mil/News/Speeches-and-Testimonies/Article-View/Article/1859890/russian-and-chinese-nuclear-modernization-trends/

[74] U.S. House Select Committee. (1999, January 3). U.S. national security and military/commercial concerns with the People's Republic of China [Report]. U.S. Congress, House of Representatives. http://www.access.gpo.gov/congress/house/hr105851-html/ch2bod.html#anchor4 309987

[75] Yesin, V. (2012). *On China's nuclear potential without underestimation or exaggeration.* Asian Arms Control Project. p. 3. http://www.scribd.com/doc/98667133/ YESIN-China-s-Nuclear-Potential

[76] Quoted in National Institute for Public Policy. (2014, September). *Section II. Minimum deterrence: Fragile hope of a constant benign threat environment* [authors redacted]. p. 48. https://www.esd.whs.mil/Portals/54/Documents/FOID/Reading%20Room/Other/Litigation%20Release%20-%20Section%20II%20Minimum%20Deterrence%20Fragile%20Hope.pdf

[77] Pincus, W. (2003, February 20). U.S. explores developing low-yield nuclear weapons. *Washington Post.* https://www.washingtonpost.com/archive/politics/2003/02/20/us-explores-developing-low-yield-nuclear-weapons/3ea99155-18a2-4065-8789-a578eb10e65e/?utm_term=.8d80d4610a11.

[78] Quoted in Schneider, M. (2009, July 1). The nuclear doctrine and forces of the People's Republic of China. *Comparative Strategy*, 28(3), p. 257. http://dx.doi.org/10.1080/01495930903025276.

[79] Ibid.

[80] Schneider, M. B. (2007, November). *The nuclear doctrine and forces of the People's Republic of China.* National Institute Press. p. 21. http://www.nipp.org/wp-content/uploads/2014/12/China-nuclear-final-pub.pdf.

[81] Ibid.

[82] CIA, National Intelligence Council, "China: Possible Nuclear Artillery Test," National Intelligence Digest, CPAS NID 95-0214CX, September 14, 1995, p. 10. Partially declassified and released under FOIA to National Security Archive.

[83] Stephen Pifer, "Stop the low-yield Trident nuclear warhead," The Hill, June 8, 2019.

84 Howe, J. R. (n.d.). Potential military utility of Russian employment of advanced technology nuclear weapons in Europe—Implications for US extended deterrence. Vision Centric, Inc.

85 "Opening Remarks of Ranking Member Turner," House Armed Services Committee, June 4, 2019, https://republicans-armedservices.house.gov/news/opening-statements/opening-remarks-ranking-member-turner-3

86 For the best and most comprehensive assessment of EMP threats, see the 2017 and earlier unclassified EMP Commission reports at www.firstempcommission.org

87 EMP Commission. (2004). Report of the Commission to assess the threat to the United States from electromagnetic pulse (EMP) attack, Volume I: Executive report, pp. 1–3; Graham, W. R. (2008, July 10). Testimony before the House Armed Services Committee [transcript of speech], pp. 4–7; Smith, G. (1997, July 16). Electromagnetic pulse threats. Testimony before the House National Security Committee [Transcript of speech]; Wilson, C. (2008, July 21). High altitude electromagnetic pulse (HEMP) and high power microwave (HPM) devices: Threat assessments. Congressional Research Service. p. 7.

88 EMP Commission. (2017, July). Assessing the threat from EMP attack: Executive report and EMP Commission chairman's report. www.firstempcommission.org

89 Electromagnetic pulse threats to U.S. military and civilian infrastructure: Hearing before the Military Research and Development Subcommittee of the Committee on Armed Services, 106th Cong. (1999), p. 78. https://babel.hathitrust.org/cgi/pt?id=pst.0000046309648&view=1up&seq=3

90 Threat posed by electromagnetic pulse (EMP) attack: Hearing before the Armed Forces Committee, 110th Cong. (2008), pp. 8–9. https://fas.org/irp/congress/2008_hr/emp.pdf

91 Electromagnetic pulse threats to U.S. military and civilian infrastructure: Hearing before the Military Research and Development Subcommittee of the Committee on Armed Services, 106th Cong. (1999), p. 68. https://babel.hathitrust.org/cgi/pt?id=pst.000046309648&view=1up&seq=3

92 National Intelligence Council. (1999, September). *Foreign Missile Developments and the Ballistic Missile Threat Through 2015.* National Intelligence Estimate. CIA. p. 4. https://fas.org/irp/threat/missile/nie99msl.htm; See also the NIE of December 2001 and National Air and Space Intelligence Center. (2017). *2017 Ballistic and Cruise Missile Threat Report.* Defense Intelligence Ballistic Missile Analysis Committee. https://fas.org/irp/threat/missile/bm-2017.pdf

93 Lethality is calculated as the ratio of the lethal area of the weapon against the area of uncertainty about where the weapon might impact, as derived from the missile's circular area probable (CEP—the radius of a circle wherein the warhead has a 50% probability of impacting). For example, a 20 kt warhead with a CEP of 15 km has a 50% chance of striking anywhere within a radius of 15 km around the aimpoint, an area of about 700 km^2. If the lethal radius of the warhead is 3 km (about the range for 5 psi overpressure from a 20 kt warhead), then lethal area is

about 28 km², or merely 4% of the 700 km² area of uncertainty around the aimpoint where the warhead might impact. Since the odds of placing the warhead within the CEP of 15 km is 50%, the odds that the warhead will place its lethal area on target is the ratio of the warhead's lethal area against the area enclosed by the warhead's CEP, halved, or about 2%. The same calculations apply to biological and chemical weapons.

[94] Director for Strategic Plans and Policy. (2000, June). *Joint vision 2020.* Joint Chiefs of Staff. p. 3; Secretary of Defense. (2001, September 30). *Quadrennial defense review.* U.S. Department of Defense. p. 30; see also the *National Defense Strategy* (2018) that replaces the *Quadrennial Defense Review.*

[95] Electromagnetic pulse threats to U.S. military and civilian infrastructure: Hearing before the Military Research and Development Subcommittee of the Committee on Armed Services, 106th Cong. (1999), p. 78. https://babel.hathitrust.org/cgi/pt?id=pst.000046309648&view=1up&seq=3

[96] Threat posed by electromagnetic pulse (EMP) attack: Hearing before the Armed Forces Committee, 110th Cong. (2008), pp. 8–9. https://fas.org/irp/congress/2008_hr/emp.pdf

[97] Electromagnetic pulse threats to U.S. military and civilian infrastructure: Hearing before the Military Research and Development Subcommittee of the Committee on Armed Services, 106th Cong. (1999), pp. 79–81. https://babel.hathitrust.org/cgi/pt?id=pst.000046309648&view=1up&seq=3

[98] Ibid., p. 68.

[99] For a more comprehensive assessment of EMP attack scenarios, see the EMP Commission report *Nuclear EMP attack scenarios and combined arms cyber warfare* (July 2017).

[100] Defense Threat Reduction Agency. (2000, April). *NBC scenarios: 2002–2010.* DTRA Advanced Systems and Concepts Office and NDU Center for Counterproliferation Research. p. vii.

[101] Defense Threat Reduction Agency. (2001, April). *High altitude nuclear detonations (HAND) against low earth orbit satellites* ("HALEOS"). p. 4. https://fas.org/spp/military/program/asat/haleos.pdf

[102] Ibid., p. 5.

[103] Edwards, S. J. A. (1997). The threat of high altitude electromagnetic pulse to Force XXI. *National Security Studies Quarterly 3*(4), pp. 61–80.

[104] Ibid., pp. 62–63.

[105] Spencer, J. (2000, May 26). *America's vulnerability to a different nuclear threat: An electromagnetic pulse.* Heritage Foundation. https://www.heritage.org/defense/report/americas-vulnerability-different-nuclear-threat-anelectromagnetic-pulse

[106] Ibid.

[107] Pry, P. V. (1990). Nuclear wars: Exchanges and outcomes. Crane Russak. 24-27; Electromagnetic pulse threats to U.S. military and civilian infrastructure: Hearing before the Military Research and Development Subcommittee of the

Committee on Armed Services, 106th Cong. (1999), p. 77. https://babel.hathitrust.org/cgi/pt?id=pst.000046309648&view=1up&seq=3

[108] Ibid., p. 78.

[109] Ibid., pp. 67–68.

[110] Sanger, D., & Baker, P. (2010, April 5). Obama limits when U.S. would use nuclear arms. *New York Times.* https://www.nytimes.com/2010/04/06/world/06arms.html

[111] Ibid.

[112] National Review Symposium. (2010, April 7). *Nuclear posturing.* National Review Online. https://www.nationalreview.com/2010/04/nuclear-posturing-nro-symposium/

[113] U.S. Department of Energy. (2015, October 21). In 20th year, Stockpile Stewardship Program celebrated as one of nation's greatest achievements in science and security [Press release]. https://www.energy.gov/nnsa/articles/20th-year-stockpile-stewardship-program-celebrated-one-nation-s

[114] Borger, J. (2013, April 21). Obama accused of nuclear U-turn as guided weapons plan emerges. *The Guardian.* https://www.theguardian.com/world/2013/apr/21/obama-accused-nuclear-guided-weapons-plan

[115] Mount, A. (2018, February 2). Trump's troubling nuclear plan: How it hastens the rise of a more dangerous world. *Foreign Affairs.* https://www.foreignaffairs.com/articles/2018-02-02/trumps-troubling-nuclear-plan

[116] Stephen Andreasen, "Trump is quietly leading us closer to nuclear disaster," Washington Post, June 26, 2019.

Index